Love in Action

Love in Action

Catholic Social Teaching for Every Church

Simon Cuff

scm press

Published in 2019 by SCM Press
Editorial office 3rd Floor, Invicta House,
108–114 Golden Lane,
London EC1Y 0TG, UK
www.scmpress.co.uk

SCM Press is an imprint of Hymns Ancient & Modern Ltd
(a registered charity)

Hymns Ancient & Modern® is a registered trademark of
Hymns Ancient & Modern Ltd
13A Hellesdon Park Road, Norwich, Norfolk NR6 5DR, UK

British Library Cataloguing in Publication data

A catalogue record for this book is available
from the British Library

978 0 334 05793 2

Typeset by Manila Typesetting Company
Printed and bound by CPI Group (UK) Ltd

Contents

For all whose voices remain unheard.

Acknowledgements

I would like to thank all at SCM Press, and especially David Shervington for his guidance and support. Likewise, the staff at the British Library, and for all those others whose work has been relied on that remain unnoticed. I rely so much on my family and the prayers of my cell group, Carol, John and Di. My colleagues and students at St Mellitus are too many and too wonderful to name, especially those who have helped shape my thoughts on some of the ideas found here through conversation and teaching. I would particularly like to thank Fr Lincoln Harvey for his encouragement, and my tutees for their prayers: Andy, Natasha, David, Gary, Sarah, Mike, Phillipa, Davidson and Rachel. This book stems from an engagement with Catholic Social Teaching that has been a consistent feature of my adult life, since Philip Kennedy, Fr Peter Groves, Bishop Allen Shin, Mthr Jenn Strawbridge, Fr Andrew Davis and others opened my eyes to the possibilities of Catholicism for engaging with the world and living the Christian faith afresh. I would like to thank all those who have taught me so much at Citizens UK through community organizing, and to whom many of the practical ideas here are indebted, especially Stefan Baskerville, Matthew Bolton, Peter Brierley, Marzena Cichon-Balcerowicz, Charlotte Fischer, George Gabriel, Daniel Mackintosh and more besides. Zrinka Bralo at Migrants Organise remains a persistent source of challenge and inspiration. Fr Sean Connolly, Sr Josephine Canny OA, Selina Stone and especially Fr Angus Ritchie of the Centre for Theology and Community have persistently challenged, cajoled and taught me what it means to put the demands of the Gospel into action, and never to settle for anything less than an advance on justice in all that we do. This book would have been impossible without the support of Fr Jack Noble. All mistakes remain my own.

Introduction

In 1911, a young Belgian priest knocked on the door of 425 Mile End Road in London with a sense of trepidation. He was seeking Ben Tillett, the leader of the famous Dock Strike of 1889 which had seen London's docks grind to a standstill. A standstill resolved through the mediation of the Roman Catholic Archbishop of Westminster, Cardinal Manning.

Fr Cardijn was right to be anxious. 'Ben Tillett', he later wrote, 'was no friend of Roman collars.'[1] Ben Tillett wasn't at home, but when the two met later that afternoon, his initial interrogation of Fr Cardijn ended with the exclamation: 'The Catholic Church is a clever church. The Church of England would never send its priests to study worker organizations.'

Times have changed. Even before the publication of *Faith in the City* in 1985, the Church of England had begun to explore the issues that affect the lives of working people as well as those seeking or unable to work.[2] At the press conference announcing that Justin Welby would be the 105th Archbishop of Canterbury, he responded to a question from the Catholic periodical *The Tablet*: 'I have gained and learned so much from the Roman Catholic Church. I have learnt much from Catholic spirituality and from the glorious and – if I may say so to *The Tablet* – far too well-hidden structure of Catholic Social Teaching, which surprisingly few Catholics know about, let alone others.'[3]

Catholic Social Teaching has been described as the Roman Catholic Church's best kept secret.[4] It is a rich body of thought, the fruit of the Roman Catholic Church carefully applying the demands of the Gospel in the midst of ever-changing social and political contexts. It finds its origins in Europe at the end of the nineteenth century and continues to be worked out today, with recent interventions by Pope Francis developing this body of teaching and reflection on how the Gospel is to be preached in an increasingly globalized world.

At its heart, Catholic Social Teaching is about the restoration and reconciliation of relationships which Christ brings. The Archbishop of Canterbury describes it as 'the applied outworking of the good news of Jesus Christ in terms of social structures and social justice'.[5]

Justin Welby's interest in Catholic Social Teaching isn't new. As is obvious from the tribute he has paid this body of thought, Catholic Social Teaching isn't only for members of the Roman Catholic Church. It is, the Archbishop of Canterbury notes, a 'series of brilliant reflections on the nature of a functional and just society'.[6]

Jesus famously said that no one lights a lamp only to hide it under a bushel.[7] The aim of this book is to make the structure of Catholic Social Teaching a little less well hidden, and a little more widely known among Christians from every denomination. We will try to make sure that the light of Catholic Social Teaching is well and truly realized across Christian communities. We will explore the origins, nature and structure of Catholic Social Thought, before seeing how this body of thought might be applied to every church context in order to build churches which are truly flourishing places of holy community.

Catholic Social Teaching stems from a foundational encyclical written in 1891, often referred to by its Latin title *Rerum Novarum* ('of new things'). An encyclical is a letter written by the Pope, more normally addressed to those bishops in communion with the Holy See, but often intended to impact a wider audience by setting out a body of teaching on whatever matter the Pope writes. The encyclical *Rerum Novarum* enjoys an almost mythic status in the world of Catholic Social Teaching.[8]

The 'new things' in the title of *Rerum Novarum* are the sweeping social and economic changes which were occupying the minds and lives of many in newly industrialized Western nations at the end of the nineteenth century. Standing in the first decades of the twenty-first century, we find ourselves in the midst of similarly widespread social and economic flux. In this context, the insights of Catholic Social Teaching are especially pertinent. They have much to offer every Church as churches try to negotiate and build up the body of Christ in the midst of sweeping social and economic change.

However, the 'new things' of *Rerum Novarum* didn't appear in a vacuum. There isn't the space in this book to trace all of the influences which led to its publication in 1891.

Instead, in Chapter 1 we'll consider three important figures who laid the groundwork for the first document of Catholic Social Teaching and provide the *background* of its emergence and development. Two of these three we have met already: Cardinal Henry Edward Manning and Cardinal Joseph Cardijn. We will explore Cardinal Manning's role in the industrial dispute which brought London's docks to a halt in 1889, events which many point to as being a significant point of origin for Catholic Social Thought. We'll then consider Cardinal Cardijn's contribution to this body of teaching, especially through the foundation of the Young Christian Worker movement. We'll discuss the lessons he learned in his studies of industrialized Europe and conversations with Ben Tillett and others on how to organize communities in order for just and flourishing relationships across communities. Finally, we'll discover the importance of the thought of St Thomas Aquinas in the theoretical background to Catholic Social Teaching. It will become clear that Catholic Social Teaching is not just a strange add-on to the life and thought of the Catholic Church, but arises from the outwork of other areas of that life. It isn't the 'leftie, trendy vicar stuff, a recipe for Marxism with a pointy roof'[9] that some critics claim, but arises out of Catholic reflection on the Christian life, human life in all its fullness.

As an example of this life, and a reminder that it is not reserved just for male clerics, this chapter will also briefly consider the life and writing of Dorothy Day and her association with the Catholic Worker movement. In contrast to the other three figures in this chapter, she stands not so much behind Catholic Social Teaching as at its vanguard. She lived on the front line ministering among the people whose lives Catholic Social Teaching at its best seeks to transform. Her life and application of Catholic Social Teaching serves as another example of how this thought might be applied practically in order to help bring about the flourishing of fully human lives to which we are called.

Catholic Social Teaching has developed out of more than a century of reflection on the demands of this Christian life on ever-changing social and political conditions. Arising out of this reflection, various principles have been distilled which enable the application of Catholic Social Teaching to every church and context.

These principles are:

- The fundamental nature of human dignity.
- The Common Good.
- Solidarity.
- Subsidiarity.
- Social sin.
- The preferential option for the poor.

Our subsequent chapters will explore each of these principles in detail. Each chapter will seek to explain one of the principles of Catholic Social Teaching in the context in which it occurs within the documents which make up this body of thought. We will consider each principle's scriptural basis and any other theological source that lies behind each idea.

The *inalienable dignity* of each and every human being has its basis in the fact of our creation by and in the image of God. The *Common Good* is that which builds up the entire human race. The relationships between each of us make up the *solidarity* which strengthens the human race and builds up the body of Christ. The relationships within and across that race and body, and the intermediary groups which mediate between the individual and the whole, constitute *subsidiarity*, which keeps the power of decision-making close to those affected by any decision to be made. Where these decisions are exercised poorly or selfishly, or in the interest of certain individuals or parts of the body, we see the effect of *social sin*. Such sin is part of the world of competing interests in which we live, where conflicting claims and interests can be made on the same resources. In deciding between such claims, the *preferential option for the poor* reminds the whole of the human race that focusing on the poorest members of that race enables the flourishing of all. It should be obvious that in combination these principles strengthen the flourishing of the entire human race, and enable every member to live out the abundance of human life to which God wills us all. This is as true of the body of Christ as of the human race as a whole.

Acting in such a way as to enable this flourishing is easier said than done. Two concluding chapters look at how these principles can be applied in Christian life and across our churches. Chapter 8 looks at the process of deciding how best to act in order to contribute to the flourishing of the entire body of Christ and human race. The focus of the chapter is the principle of theological reflection which finds its basis in an aspect of Cardinal Cardijn's reflective practice – 'see, judge, act'. This is the model of observation, reflection and action which guides how Catholic Social Thought is put into practice. Here we once again see the importance of St Thomas Aquinas to the field of Catholic Social Thought, as behind this process of deliberation toward practical steps lies St Thomas' teaching on prudence and practical action.

The aim of Catholic Social Teaching is to strengthen the relationships between people in order to enable and increase the flourishing of every person. In Chapter 9 we ask how these principles can be applied not just to enable the flourishing of each and every person, but each and every church community. Much of what we discuss will be applicable to other institutions which mediate relationships between and across the whole of humankind. However, we'll focus on what it means to belong to church communities which live as examples of this flourishing. We'll ask how the principles of Catholic Social Teaching can be applied in the daily life of churches, parishes and Christian communities to enrich the entire body of Christ and so that communities of genuine human flourishing might be celebrated and built up.

There are many ways to introduce new readers to the depths of wisdom to be encountered within the social teaching of the Catholic Church. It is possible to do so historically or chronologically and unpack the development of that thought over time. It is possible to take each document in which Catholic Social Teaching is found in turn, and distil what contribution such teaching might have today. Both have validity and are approaches which have been taken by others.[10] We have opted instead to introduce Catholic Social Teaching through the principles distilled within Catholic Social Teaching itself and set out above.

This offers us a systematic approach to unpack and apply these principles of flourishing. The main advantage of doing so is that this enables their practical application most directly. Catholic Social Teaching isn't meant to be locked away in a library or parish archive, but shared widely so that all people of good will might further the cause of human flourishing.

In what follows, gendered language is left as it is found in the official translations. In almost every case 'man' refers to all humankind, regardless of gender. Where this is not the case, and a particular expression of gender is the subject of discussion, this has been made clear. The persistent use of 'man' and 'him' to denote all of humankind is more than unfortunate, but it proved too disruptive to the sense of the underlying text to alter the original or to make clear by use of 'sic' where gendered language was intended to refer to all humanity.

There are disadvantages to any approach. It is in reality impossible to isolate the principles from each other, and we shall see political attempts to do so lose something of each principle. They are, as the *Compendium of Social Doctrine* describes, to be 'appreciated in their unity, interrelatedness and articulation'.[11] Throughout, it is important to remember that the principles are based on and related to each other, in the way a Russian doll interlocks or different pillars of a structure combine to make a whole.

By focusing on the principles, we also risk losing some of the sense of historical development of Catholic Social Teaching as the twentieth century proceeded. However, as we chart the development of each principle a historical picture will begin to unfold. At the beginning of its history, we see Catholic Social Teaching's origins in the Church's response to broadly external pressures – the pastoral challenge of the working conditions of many thousands of Catholic faithful and the political challenges of revolutionary communism and socialism. As the century went on, we see how such external pressures shifted and changed, from conditions within nations to disparities between nations and continents, and how Catholic Social Teaching responded with new applications of this vision of flourishing human life. We also see how the nature of such pressures changed too, from being predominantly external at the outset of Catholic Social Teaching, to the more internal challenge coming from the faithful and from among clergy and theologians within the Church.

We see this most of all in the rise of Liberation Theology in the second half of the twentieth century. Liberation Theology is the theological movement arising out of the particular context of South America as it began to move and think past its European heritage and faced the new social challenges of the latter half of the century. It arose in response to the detrimental impact of globalization, rising inequality and deepening poverty among some sections of Latin American society.

Early developments in Catholic Social Teaching sought to spell out clearly how a renewed and reinvigorated Christian life could avoid the threat of social unrest posed by politically revolutionary forces on the one hand, while meeting the challenge of social need those forces set out to meet on the other.

We shall see how in the latter part of the twentieth century, in the wake of Liberation Theology, Catholic Social Teaching increasingly sought to mediate between perceived excesses of that theology. Frequently we see more radical and potentially demanding claims of Liberation Theology, mediated into a form which can be accepted more readily by the whole Church as a basis for the flourishing of human life. It remains to be seen how and whether these accommodations preserve the thrust of the insight of Liberation Theology, and whether they preserve the commitment for the flourishing of all human society, especially the poorest.

We shall see below that Catholic Social Teaching seeks to do exactly that, but that even the documents of Catholic Social Teaching must always be brought back to those principles which it has gifted the Church. It is a constant task to enable the flourishing of the whole body of Christ and the whole of human life. It is a constant task to check that the mechanisms with which the poorest are made poor are not allowed to persist. As one document of Catholic Social Teaching puts it, it is the constant task of 'building a human community where men can live truly human lives, free from discrimination on account of race, religion or nationality, free from servitude to other men or to natural forces which they cannot yet control satisfactorily. It involves building a human community where liberty is not an idle word.'[12]

In a world which seems to be increasingly divided and in which inequality between rich and poor seems to be on the rise, the need to build the Church and reunite the human family according to the principles of Catholic Social Teaching has never been more pressing. If, by introducing the principles of Catholic Social Teaching to a small number of those who have not encountered them before, this book can be a very small contribution to the flourishing of the whole Church and human family, the strengthening of human relationship and the overcoming of false divisions we have made for ourselves, it will have achieved its aim.

The Second Vatican Council

Before we begin our exploration of Catholic Social Teaching, we first need to describe a significant event in the life of the Roman Catholic Church, whose influence was felt across many Christian denominations. This event is the Second Vatican Council, which had huge repercussions for the teaching of the Church and for the theology and practice of many Christian denominations.

Pope John XXIII called the Second Vatican Council, a meeting of the Bishops of the Church, to consider the nature of the Church in modernity. After John XXIII's death, Pope Paul VI continued the process his predecessor had begun.

The Council met between 1962 and 1965 to address a number of pastoral and theological issues raised by the modern world. It issued a series of decrees and constitutions on a number of topics. Pope John XXIII is reported to have said that he called the Council in order to 'throw open the windows of the church and let the fresh air of the spirit blow through'. The word '*aggiornamento*' became associated with the proceedings of the Council. It means 'to refresh' or 'bring up to date'.

The Second Vatican Council would bring about extensive change within the life and liturgy of the Church. Its interpretation is still a matter of debate within the Roman Catholic Church today. For our purposes, it issued the Pastoral Constitution on the Church in the Modern World (*Gaudium et Spes*), which begins with this clarion call: 'The joys and the hopes, the griefs and the anxieties of the men of this age, especially those who are poor or in any way afflicted, these are the joys and hopes, the griefs and anxieties of the followers of Christ.'[13]

The atmosphere of theological enquiry associated with the Council would permeate throughout the Catholic world. The spirit of the Council as lived out in Latin America would be a contributing factor to the rise of Liberation Theology in the proceeding years, as we shall see when we consider the concepts of social sin and the preferential option for the poor.

The Documents of Catholic Social Teaching

Finally, in order to aid navigating subsequent chapters, the following represent the documents normally recognized as the official or 'magisterial' documents of Catholic Social Teaching. They gain this status as either letters written by the Popes intended for wide circulation, known as encyclicals; other papal documents; or those written by a number of Bishops meeting as attendees of an official meeting of the Church. In each case, we provide a brief description of the document and its date. The abbreviation it will be referred to within the footnotes appears in brackets after the title. All of the documents can be found in translation on the Vatican website (www.vatican.va).

Rerum Novarum (Rerum) [Of New Things] Leo XIII (1891)

Pope Leo XIII seeks to respond to the worsening social conditions experienced as a result of industrialization in the West. He attacks the solutions offered by socialism and suggests that a social framework based on the conceptual framework offered by St Thomas Aquinas will benefit society. He defends private property as a right (for the first time), argues for a just wage, and the right for workers to join and form trade unions.

Quadragesimo Anno (Quadragesimo) [On the Fortieth Year] Pius XI (1931)

Pope Pius' encyclical cements the status of Leo XIII's *Rerum Novarum* as the foundational encyclical of Catholic Social Teaching. Pius XI critiques the current financial system, particularly in light of the Great Depression, and reaffirms Leo's rejection of communism and socialism.

Mater et Magistra (Mater) [Mother and Teacher] John XXIII (1961)

The first truly international document of Catholic Social Teaching. John XXIII writes concerning international aid and global development, the role of the laity and the importance of just wages. He emphasizes that Catholic Social Teaching is an integral part of the Church's life.

Pacem in Terris (Pacem) [Peace on Earth] John XXIII (1963)

John XXIII's call for peace, made during the Cold War and in the midst of the nuclear arms race. An account of human rights is developed explicitly for the first time in Catholic Social Teaching in the context of the advance of 'human rights' as a concept within international law.

Dignitatis Humanae (Dignitatis) [Human Dignity] Paul VI (1965)

Pope Paul VI's first social encyclical deals with the concept of human dignity. This principle is widely regarded as the foundation of Catholic Social Teaching.

Gaudium et Spes (Gaudium) [The Joys and Hopes] Second Vatican Council (1965)

'The Pastoral Constitution on the Church in the Modern World.' *Gaudium et Spes* is a key document in the history of modern Christianity. The Council Fathers calls on the Church to read the modern world and apply Church teaching in light of the 'signs of the times'. The document deals especially with human dignity and human community.

Populorum Progressio (Populorum) [The Development of Peoples] Paul VI (1967)

Paul VI stresses the importance of global development for international peace. He suggests limits to the nature of private property, and questions the place of profit in the motives of industry. He calls on Christians to strive for justice internationally, and for the development of poorer nations.

Octogesima Adveniens (Octogesima) [On the Eightieth Year] Paul VI 1971

This encyclical further enshrines *Rerum Novarum* as the foundational document of Catholic Social Teaching. We see the place of the environment and ecological issues as an explicit focus for the first time, while also focusing on new social problems arising in the course of urbanization.

Laborem Exercens (Laborem) [On Human Work] John Paul II 1981

This encyclical reflects on the dignity of human labour, and the role that work can have in enhancing human dignity. John Paul II offers a critique of both capitalism and Marxism, while addressing the rights of workers, particularly women, and reinforcing the importance of trade unions. The theme of solidarity is highlighted as especially important within the workplace.

Sollicitudo Rei Socialis (Sollicitudo) [The Social Concern of the Church] John Paul II 1987

This encyclical sees the synthesis of magisterial Catholic teaching and Liberation Theology, within the incorporation of two insights from Liberation Theology in modified form: 'structures of sin' and the preferential option for the poor. There is a special emphasis on the developing world.

Centesimus Annus (Centesimus) [The One Hundredth Year] John Paul II 1991

Written shortly after the fall of the Berlin Wall, John Paul surveys the events of the last century and affirms the importance of human dignity and human rights. He emphasizes the destiny of goods to serve people's needs and condemns unbridled capitalism. His reflections are especially important as a critique following the demise of Eastern state 'communism' at a time when capitalism was thought to have triumphed.

Evangelium Vitae (Evangelium) [Gospel of Life] John Paul II 1995

John Paul II's encyclical is most famous for its moral teaching on subjects such as abortion and euthanasia. He employs 'structures of sin' from within Liberation Theology within the course of these moral arguments. This encyclical is an extended reflection on the foundational role that human dignity should play in our dealings with every other person.

Compendium of Social Doctrine of the Church Pontifical Council of Justice and Peace 2004

The *Compendium* combines more than a century of official reflection on the Social Teaching of the Church into one exhaustive document. It distils the principles of Catholic Social Teaching (which are the basis of this book) from the encyclicals and other pronouncements of Catholic Social Teaching.

Caritas in Veritate (Caritas) [Charity in Truth] Benedict XVI 2009

Written after the financial crisis, Pope Benedict reviews social development and reflects on the ethics of business in light of the economic crisis. Benedict XVI is rightly hailed as the most 'theological' Pope of the modern papacy. He demonstrates this theological acumen here, and deepens the theological basis of Catholic Social Teaching.

Evangelii Gaudium (Evangelii Gaudium) [Joy of the Gospel] Francis 2013

An exhortation focused on the importance of sharing the Gospel. The second half focuses on the social aspects of the Christian faith, and re-emphasizes the importance of the just wage and human solidarity. Francis also stresses the importance of social development.

Laudato Si (Laudato) [On Care for our Common Home] Francis 2015

An extended reflection on the environment and economic inequality, very possibly timed to be released in time for the international conference on climate change taking place that year in Paris (which led to the Paris Agreement on Climate Change). The encyclical was hugely controversial among many conservatives, sceptical about climate change, both Catholic and non-Catholic. Francis also received condemnation for his challenge to the economic status quo. In so doing, he maintains a strong tradition of prophetic denunciation of economic excess where it is not in accordance with the Common Good, as we shall see from what follows.

Notes

1 Cardijn, J., 'Worker organisation in England', in *Revue Sociale Catholique* (November–December 1911) (available at: http://www.josephcardijn.com/worker-organisation-in-england) (accessed 28 August 2018).

2 Archbishop of Canterbury's Commission on Urban Priority Areas, *Faith in the City: A Call for Action by Church and Nation* (London: Church House Publishing, 1985). For a summary of Anglican social teaching, see Brown, M. (ed.), *Anglican Social Theology: Renewing the Vision Today* (London: Church House Publishing, 2014). For the

political role of Archbishops of Canterbury in recent years, see Gover, D., *Turbulent Priests: The Archbishop of Canterbury in Contemporary English Politics* (London: Theos, 2011) available at: https://www.theos-thinktank.co.uk/cmsfiles/archive/files/Reports/TheosTurbulentPriests2.pdf (accessed 11 June 2018).

3 Lamb, C., 'Archbishop means business', in *The Tablet* (November 2012), reproduced at: http://www.thinkinganglicans.org.uk/archives/005744.html (accessed 28 August 2018).

4 DeBerri, E. P., Jug, J. E. with Henriot, P. J. and Schulthreis M. J., *Catholic Social Teaching: Our Best Kept Secret* (Maryknoll, NY: Orbis Books, 1988). Walsh, M., 'The Myth of Rerum Novarum' in *New Blackfriars* 93 No. 1044 (March 2012), 155–62 notes the 'ever-increasing inaccuracy' of this description.

5 Welby, J., *Reimagining Britain: Foundations for Hope* (London: Bloomsbury, 2018), 35.

6 Welby, *Reimagining*, 35.

7 Matthew 5.15.

8 Walsh, 'Myth', 155.

9 Welby, *Reimagining*, 36.

10 Brady, B., *Essential Catholic Social Thought* (Maryknoll, NY: Orbis Books, 2008), 1. Outlines four usual ways: reading the documents in their entirety; reading excerpts; reading summaries; reading the principles.

11 Pontifical Council for Justice and Peace, *Compendium of the Social Doctrine of the Church* (London: Bloomsbury 2004), §162.

12 Paul VI, *Populorum Progressio* ('On the Development of Peoples') 47 (26 March 1967), available at: http://w2.vatican.va/content/paul-vi/en/encyclicals/documents/hf_p-vi_enc_26031967_populorum.html (accessed 13 June 2018).

13 Pastoral Constitution on the Church in the Modern World *Gaudium et Spes* (promulgated by His Holiness Pope Paul VI, 7 December 1965), available at: http://www.vatican.va/archive/hist_councils/ii_vatican_council/documents/vat-ii_const_19651207_gaudium-et-spes_en.html (accessed 2 November 2017).

I

Background

Ideas are always lived out in the people whose lives are ordered or affected by them. Ideas shape, and are shaped by, people. In Catholic life and thought, one of the roles of the saints is to put into personal form the Christian life, so that we see more easily in them how we might live that same life, 'their great example lends us courage, their fervent prayers sustain us in all we do'.[1]

In order to understand the background which gave rise to Catholic Social Teaching, this chapter looks at the biographies of three key figures who demonstrate the reasons for the development of Catholic Social Teaching in the twentieth century, or were influential in the principles which would later be derived from that teaching. We then go on to look at one figure as she sought to apply these principles in her life and ministry, in order to begin from the outset to think about how such principles might be practically applied.

The list of figures who have inspired Catholic Social Teaching is long, and we will encounter many of the Popes and liberation theologians who have done so in the course of this book. However, these first three figures stand alone as figures with a unique contribution as examples of the social and economic issues which gave rise to Catholic Social Teaching; as examples of the influence of a charismatic ministry bearing fruit in the development of Catholic Social Thought; and as part of the theoretical basis to which much of Catholic life and thought continues to be indebted. These three are Cardinal Henry Edward Manning (1808–92), Cardinal Joseph Cardijn (1882–1967) and St Thomas Aquinas (1225–74). Finally, we will see how

Dorothy Day (1897–1980) gives us a powerful example of the fruits of Catholic Social Teaching, and the lives of those for whom and with whom Catholic Social Teaching came about.

The choice of these figures is partly personal, as they are four figures who have helped me to understand how these principles might be applied as we live out the Christian life. There are many others who deserve inclusion here: Mgr Jack Egan (1916–2001), a priest from Chicago who combined priesthood and community organizing in a radically compelling way;[2] as well as many other laypeople, clergy, activists, Popes and theologians who have contributed to the development of this body of thought, many of whom we will encounter on the pages below. The figures focused on in this chapter have been singled out partly because each of them helps us to understand something unique of the history and practical application of Catholic Social Teaching, but also, particularly in the case of Cardinal Cardijn and St Thomas Aquinas, their contribution is less obvious or well known to those outside this field of study.

Cardinal Manning's ministry stands as an example of the social conditions which necessitated the writing of the first encyclical of Catholic Social Teaching, *Rerum Novarum*, in 1891. This document quickly, as we shall see below, gained foundational status and can rightly be seen as the original document of Catholic Social Teaching. Cardinal Manning's role in the London Dock Strike of 1889 is an important precursor to how a ministry which enacts the principles of Catholic Social Teaching might mediate between different groups in society for the benefit of the poorest in those societies. The issues raised by the strike were also influential in the content and themes of that first encyclical.

Cardinal Cardijn continued the legacy of the Catholic Church in ministry among working populations into the twentieth century. He founded the Young Christian Worker movement and was responsible for the inclusion of key themes and methods which were later to find expression in Catholic Social Teaching.

It might seem strange to include St Thomas Aquinas among our three figures. We shall see that Pope Leo XIII (1810–1903), the Pope responsible for the publication of *Rerum Novarum*, placed a great deal of importance on the thought of St Thomas Aquinas as a means of fostering relationships within human society. We shall see elements of Aquinas' thought which will be applied and developed within Catholic Social Teaching. The legacy of St Thomas here acts as a reminder of the relationships between Catholic Social Teaching and every other aspect of Catholic life and thought. He is a helpful reminder that Catholic Social Teaching isn't a strange add-on or sideshow for the politically left, but arises out of Catholic life as a whole. The practical application of Catholic thought to strengthen the relationships within, and contribute to the flourishing of, society within the contemporary world are the fruit of reflection that Catholic Social Teaching offers the Church as a whole.

Finally, we look at the life and witness of Dorothy Day (1897–1980). She stands not so much at the background of Catholic Social Teaching, but at its foreground and at its frontline. Reflecting on her life and witness offers us an opportunity to begin thinking about how we can practically apply the insights of Catholic Social Teaching. She will remind us from the outset of the book that our theory will only take us so far. The litmus test of any principle of Catholic Social Teaching will be its ability to inspire action, the kind of action for which Dorothy Day gained notoriety. Her example will hold us to account throughout as we unfold the principles of Catholic Social Teaching and begin to ask how these might be put into practice. She will help us as we ask how such principles might contribute to the flourishing of every church and community.

Our survey begins with Cardinal Manning, a journey which takes us to the East End of London at the end of the twentieth century. We will find ourselves faced with a community divided over the issue of fair pay, amid poor and insecure working conditions, where the effects of a prolonged strike are beginning to be felt by owner and worker alike.

Cardinal Henry Edward Manning (1808–1892)

It is difficult for us to understand the hostility towards Roman Catholics which was a feature of British life until more recently than we might realize. Today, Catholic, Anglican and Protestant alike are free to worship as they wish and are increasingly recognizing that they are more united in Christ than they are divided in history. This was not always the case.

The Reformation saw the Church of England separate itself from the Church of Rome, and left a legacy of suspicion and intolerance towards those who professed allegiance to Rome as guardian of the Catholic faith. The process by which Roman Catholics were freed to worship as they wished began in the eighteenth century and advanced greatly in 1829 with the passing of the Roman Catholic Relief Act. No longer were Roman Catholics barred from taking up political office in Westminster or from other public offices (with few exceptions). While the offices covered in these acts affected a relatively small percentage of the Roman Catholic population, its social affects were to be much greater. Catholicism was once more to be a public feature of British life.

It was not only the emancipation of Catholics that increased the public profile of Catholicism at this time. A movement within the Church of England would shortly emerge which led to a much greater interest in Catholic theology and practice. It would see Anglican clergy and theologians rediscover their shared inheritance and seek greater unity with Christians professing allegiance to Rome.

On 14 July 1833, John Keble, Professor of Poetry at the University of Oxford, preached the University's Assize sermon on the theme of 'National Apostasy'. Keble was preaching in response to the recent parliamentary intervention to reduce the number of bishops in the Church of Ireland. His sermon against State intervention in matters of national religion is thought by many to have inaugurated this movement, which became known as the 'Oxford Movement' – a religious movement within the Church of England which would lead to a rediscovery of the Catholic roots of Anglicanism.

The Oxford Movement also led to the conversion of many Anglicans to Roman Catholicism. One such figure, and our focus here, is Cardinal Henry Edward Manning. Cardinal Manning had been an Anglican priest and archdeacon, but converted to Roman Catholicism in 1851 in protest at the involvement of the Privy Council in matters of church doctrine. He was consecrated as Archbishop of Westminster in 1865, and made a Cardinal some ten years later. His time as Archbishop of Westminster was marked by a constant zeal for the growing class of urban poor, many if not most of them Catholics. He frequently addressed meetings of the growing labour movement.

Shortly before being raised to Cardinal, on 28 January 1874, he gave a lecture at the Mechanics' Institution in Leeds on 'the Dignity and Rights of Labour'. Here he spells out his commitment to the Common Good – a central feature of Catholic Social Teaching as we shall see below. Manning proclaimed: 'I conceive to be a high dictate of our duty that . . . in everything of private life, and everything of domestic and civil and political life, we have but one common interest – the welfare of our common country. If there be divergences, as there must be, as always have been, and as I fear there always will be, it seems to me that it is the duty of every one of us to strive that they should be suspended at least in every region of our public and private life wheresoever it is possible.'[3]

Here Cardinal Manning sets out a concept of the Common Good which is demanding and far-ranging. In doing so, he foreshadowed the emergence of the Common Good as a principle of Catholic Social Teaching. We will focus more on this principle as it comes to be expounded in the later documents in Chapter 3 below.

For Cardinal Manning, however, the Common Good required the suspension of conflicting interests for the sake of the whole of society, wherever possible. He recognizes, however, that there are cases where it will never be possible to reconcile competing interests. The Common Good demands as much effort as possible to put aside these conflicting interests for the sake of society as a whole.

One issue he recognized as central to the Common Good was the dignity of labour, and the importance of a social life for all workers and labourers outside of the working day for the flourishing of those workers' lives: 'If the great end of life were to multiply yards of cloth and cotton twist, and if the glory of England consists or consisted in multiplying, without stint or limit, these articles and the like at the lowest possible price, so as to undersell all the nations of the world, well, then, let us go on. But if the domestic life of the people be vital above all; if the peace, the purity of homes, the education of children, the duties of wives and mothers, the duties of husbands and of fathers, be written in the natural law of mankind, and if these things are sacred, far beyond anything that can be sold in the market – then I say, if the hours of labour resulting from the unregulated sale of a man's strength and skill shall lead to the destruction of domestic life, to the neglect of children, to turning wives and mothers into living machines, and of fathers and husbands into – what shall I say? – creatures of burden – I will not use any other word – who rise up before the sun, and come back when it is set, wearied and able only to take food and to lie down to rest – the domestic life of men exists no longer, and we dare not go on in this path.'[4]

Here we see Cardinal Manning appeal to the Catholic concept of natural law as demanding that the labour of workers is not exploited solely for profit, to 'undersell all the nations of the world'. Instead, natural law, which is more notorious as it is applied to matters of sexual ethics, is appealed to in defence of a flourishing home and family life for those in work. Work must not be so excruciating as to leave the worker unable to do anything other than 'take food and to lie down and rest'. Natural law, claims Cardinal Manning, dictates that men and women have a right to a fully domestic life – with space for family and social activity. We see already that the appeal for certain living and working conditions isn't a strange addition to the rest of Catholic life and thought, but arises out of precepts which are fundamental to it.

Cardinal Manning's concern for a decent domestic life for all working people was not limited to the balance between work and home life. He was a significant contributor to two Royal Commissions on the Housing of the Working Classes (1884) and on education (1885).

Even before his role in the Dock Strike of 1889, Cardinal Manning foreshadows themes which will later develop into the principles of Catholic Social Teaching: the Common Good and the right to a decent domestic life. The life and ministry of Cardinal Manning is often held to have been influential on the themes and writing of *Rerum Novarum*, and so on the construction of Catholic Social Teaching as a whole.

However, Cardinal Manning's notoriety as a campaigner for social justice and hero of Catholic Social Thought stems primarily from his role in the Great Dock Strike of 1889 in London's East End. From Cardinal Manning's conduct during the strike, we learn many lessons for putting faith into action today: persistence, compromise and the importance of relationship.

The dockers, many of them Irish Catholics, went on strike on 14 August 1889 over decreased rates of bonus pay, calling for a penny wage increase and minimum hours contracts. Cardinal Manning, as part of his duty of care for London's Catholic community, was one of the first public figures to intervene on their behalf.

At the beginning of September, the Lord Mayor of London brought together a committee at Mansion House including the Bishop of London and Cardinal Manning to mediate between those on strike and the dock directors. The committee was successful in settling the matter of the dispute. The dockers would receive a pay increase and an increased overtime rate, and no striking worker would be punished for their involvement in the strike. However, the dock directors and those on strike couldn't agree on when the new pay rate would start. The directors wanted to begin the new pay rates from January, and those on strike wanted them to begin from October.

Most of the Mansion House committee, including the then Bishop of London, became exasperated at this stalemate. Cardinal Manning alone demonstrated persistence. He continued to meet with the dockers and the directors when other mediators had thrown in the towel.

He continued to meet until he had taught both sides the importance of compromise to bring about an end to the strike. Eventually, he persuaded both to agree to compromise on their position and that the new rates of pay would be brought in from November. Accounts of that final meeting are electrifying: 'Unaccustomed tears glistened in the eyes of his rough and work-stained hearers as he raised his hand, and solemnly urged them not to prolong one moment more than they could help the perilous uncertainty, and the suffering of their wives and children . . . When he sat down all in the room knew in their own minds that he had won the day, and that so far as the councils were concerned that was the end of the strike – the Cardinal's peace.'[5]

How did Cardinal Manning achieve this peace? He did so through the sharing of testimony and the prioritizing of relationship. The leader of the strike, Ben Tillet, recalled the Cardinal's use of the stories of those suffering by the continuation of the strike: 'I could not withstand this gentle old man, who touched so tenderly the heart-strings of his hearers with solemn talk about the sufferings of wives and children, or impress him with a summary of social needs and economic complexities multiplying in the prolongation of the Strike. I never look back on that meeting without a sense of nightmare, but there was a final judgment and the Cardinal won.'[6]

Even more important than testimony was the Cardinal's cultivation of relationships. It was noted at the time that: 'His Eminence is looked upon by the strike leaders as one of their best friends . . . so venerable and amiable an intermediary as Cardinal Manning.'[7] Through cultivating relationships with both strikers and dock directors, he was able to influence the strike to bring it to an end with the best possible deal for the low paid, because he knew of the severity of their plight, and had earned their trust and respect to act with them for the Common Good.

Cardinal Manning's legacy was not only felt in the history of the labour movement through his part in the landmark victory during the Dockers' Strike. He is also a founding figure of Catholic Social Teaching itself through his role in bringing the conditions which lead to the writing of *Rerum Novarum* to the notice of the wider Church. This contribution led to a new era of the relationship between Catholicism and industrialized society which is the subject of this book.

News of Cardinal Manning's success at brokering a compromise between the dock workers and owners reached Rome, where he was praised for being a mediator between Church and society. We can surmise that Leo XIII was therefore aware of Manning's concern for, and relationships with, the workforce of the day. Some later commentators, however, exaggerate his role in the beginning of Catholic Social Teaching.

While panegyrics such as the following overplay his role in the writing of *Rerum Novarum*, they also demonstrate the impact that it is possible to have when the Church is at the forefront and in the midst of relations between employee and employer alike: 'He chose to die at Westminster, poor and ascetic, in frayed garments; therefore, while living, he was . . . the arbitrator in the Dock Strike, when he won for Labour, as I said then, its "Battle of Valmy" and the era of an Industrial Reformation according to Pope Leo's doctrine of a "living wage" was inaugurated. That Magna Charta, which defined the duties and rights of economic justice, owed its inception to Manning.'[8]

Cardinal Joseph Cardijn (1882–1967)

Joseph Cardijn was the founder of the 'Jeunesse Ouvrière Chrétienne' or 'Young Christian Workers', a group often known by their acronyms Jocists, JOC or YCW. Throughout his life Cardijn sought to integrate ecclesial and industrial life so that those in work might remain in the Church, and that those in the Church might remain close to those working and not become a Church of the comfortable elite. His life offers us an example of how to integrate Church teaching and everyday life.

He also had a direct influence on Catholic Social Thought, with the practical method of decision-making (see, judge, act) developed within the JOC being incorporated into official Catholic Social Teaching by John XXIII in *Mater et Magistra*. We shall consider that method in Chapter 8 below. In this section, we will explore his example of how to integrate principles of Catholic Social Teaching into everyday life.

Born in Belgium to a working family, Joseph Cardijn entered seminary in 1896, at the age of 14. Returning home he realized the growing distance between himself and his school friends, who were forced to work in intolerable conditions within local factories. He later recalled seeing these young people: 'From that moment onwards I was haunted, haunted for life, by the call: to save the working class. I could see that endless procession of young people, thirteen or fourteen years old, forced to leave school in order to work in corrupt conditions. They had been given an entirely false idea of work, of girls, of dates, of love, of marriage.'[9]

It was these false ideas, and the fact that the same children had stopped going to Church once they entered the factory, that inspired Cardijn's life's work: 'They had entered the factory and were already corrupted, lost. They no longer went to church. I vowed that this would not go on. That's how the J. O. C. started.'[10]

Cardinal Cardijn was ordained priest in 1906, and shortly afterward began teaching at a small seminary in Belgium. In the summer of 1911, he travelled to England to study the conditions of the working classes there. While there, he met Ben Tillett, the leader of the Dock Strike we have already encountered above in the life of Cardinal Manning.

Tillett exercised a profound influence on the young priest. He was later to remark: 'A talk with Ben Tillett . . . did me more good than a retreat.'[11] We can already see the seeds of what would become the JOC in his analysis of Tillett's method of trade union organization: 'Two feelings have crystallized his aspirations and, like two stars, have guided his efforts for a better future. Firstly, he wants to create an organization as strong, as wide, as unified as possible, in which the workers of the whole world can feel the solidarity of their interests and the invincible might of their union. Then he wants every worker in particular to undertake the education of his own individuality, to raise it morally and intellectually in order to get a feel for the pressing needs for greater well-being and justice. This twofold action makes a harmonious whole.'[12]

Cardijn would develop this 'twofold action' within the JOC – the desire to create an organization that is 'as strong, as wide, as unified as possible', with each worker continuing their education to heighten their own moral and intellectual awareness.

He observed within Ben Tillett's trade union movement how leaders were identified and developed: 'The psychology of a leader is very complex: an impulsive spirit often moved at first by a vague sense of aspiration for greater well-being, depressed by the misery and injustice around him; only gradually, through meeting with kindred spirits in books, in visits, in conversations, does the means become real and the mind becomes aware of the lessons of experience, of the route to follow and the formula to adopt.'[13]

We see here why Cardijn would give a role to continuing education within the JOC, 'meeting with kindred spirits in books, in visits, in conversation' as a means to develop leaders. We also see the seeds of his 'see-judge-act' method, as the leader develops through observation of the conditions around him, judges them through this process of continuing education, before a course of action comes to mind, 'the route to follow and the formula to adopt'.

In 1912, he was appointed curate of a parish in Brussels with a large population of factory workers. Early commentators note he cut a very different clerical figure to the clergy they were used to: 'The visiting priests they had known always asked,

"Do you still go to Mass? Did you make your Easter duties?" The approach of the new curate offered novelty. "A cigarette? Where do you work? What's it like there? How did you get the job? Are there prospects?"'[14]

He set about organizing the working population into associations and trade unions, firstly the young women who were given to his charge.[15] He began a study group which was administered by the women themselves, and instituted a small membership charge so that the women made extra effort to make the most out of joining the group. Later a similar group emerged of young working men, jealous of the opportunities for development the young women were enjoying thanks to the organization of Fr Cardijn.

These were not study groups for study's sake. Cardijn himself declared in the Manual of the JOC: 'The study circle without works is a dead study circle. The study circle is not just a teaching business. It communicates a faith, a faith enthusiastic for social, moral, and religious action and organization.'[16]

A key feature of these groups is the autonomy for individual members whose membership must be 'freely chosen and even desired as a privilege . . . My personal advice is that we must advocate the fullest autonomy possible.'[17] The members of the study groups demonstrated this autonomy as they 'co-operate in seeking, gathering together, bring all that other matter, living and lived: the facts, the inquiries, the books, the conferences, the lessons'.[18] This autonomy and collaboration within a smaller organization, which develops capacity to act within society at large, becomes a key feature of later Catholic Social Teaching through the principle of subsidiarity, as we shall see in Chapter 5 below.

After the First World War, these groups were initially known as 'La Jeunesse Syndicaliste' (the Young Trade Unionists), but were renamed in 1925 the Young Christian Workers (JOC), in which year the movement was given the blessing of Pope Pius XI.

Fr Cardijn's support for workers and working communities led to a flurry of complaints that he was little more than a socialist. These complaints led to the organization being banned by the local Church hierarchy. Cardijn therefore travelled to Rome to seek approval of the work he was doing. He is reported to have exclaimed to Pope Pius XI that he wanted to kill himself to save the working masses, to which the Pope responded: 'At last! Here is someone who talks to me of the saving of the masses. Everyone else talks to me of the elite.'[19] The ban was lifted and the JOC spread first to France in 1927 and then across the world, declining in numbers and impact after the death of Cardijn, but still in existence worldwide today.[20]

We shall consider the see-judge-act method in more detail below. We now move to see what lessons can be drawn from the wider methodology of the JOC and Cardijn's vision for the integration of church and everyday life.

A key feature of the JOC was that it was lay-led and lay-directed. It was an organization of laypeople for laypeople. Emilie Arnould, a leader within JOC in Belgium, described it is an 'autonomous movement by the young workers, for the young workers; a movement of education in order that all young workers can discover and realize their vocations'.[21] We see again the importance of education as a means to inspire right action and the vocation of those young people at work.

Pius XI notes in *Quadragesimo Anno* that laypeople in similar professions are often the best evangelists of laypeople: 'The first and immediate apostles to the workers ought to be workers; the apostles to those who follow industry and trade ought to be from among them themselves.'[22] Fr Cardijn also provides a good example of the role of the clergy, according to Pius XI, as those whose duty it is 'to search diligently lay apostles both of workers and of employers, to select them with prudence, and to train and instruct them properly'.[23] The entire methodology of the JOC is the process of selecting and training lay leadership. The role of the priest both as chaplain to each JOC group and in support of the lay directors at local and regional levels is 'to raise up leaders, furnish their weapons and train them, for these are the kernel of Jocism, its head, its heart without whom no conquest is possible'.[24]

Fr Cardijn's JOC movement reminds us that the business of living out the social teaching of the Church is the task of the whole Church. More than this, it is the role of all Christian people, not the clergy alone, to be the vanguard of Christian social life and practice.

All of these lessons can be summarized in Cardijn's own reflections on the integration of ecclesial and everyday life: 'For an immense number of Christians, religion is only a private affair, something apart from their daily work. It should be its spirit, its motive power, its transformer, its supernaturalizator . . . Religion is a whole life which, like the host, should be consecrated to God. All this, so that through this life united with Christ *per ipsum*, *in ipso*, *cum ipso* [through him, in him, with him] all honour and glory may be given to him who reigns for ever and ever.'[25]

St Thomas Aquinas (1225–1274)

It might seem strange to include the life of a medieval theologian and philosopher in a book dedicated mostly to the application of Catholic thought to the contemporary social problems which have arisen since the dawn of industrialization. However, we shall see repeatedly throughout this book that Thomism – the Catholic intellectual framework deriving from the consideration and application of St Thomas' thought – lies behind many of the solutions Catholic Social Teaching offers to these problems. We shall see also that some elements of Catholic Social Teaching are derived from a Thomist intellectual framework and way of looking at the world.

In this section we shall not be describing Aquinas' life or body of thought.[26] Instead we shall see how Thomist ideas lie behind some of the background to Catholic Social Teaching and its development. We shall see too how this application of Thomist principles explains some of the features of later

Catholic Social Thought, from the living wage to the see-judge-act method of practical decision-making.

In very brief terms, Aquinas' theological system saw the application of Aristotlean thought as a means to speak theologically. In this respect he is seeking to speak well (or better) about God using the best philosophy of the day. Aristotle is an Ancient Greek philosopher whose work had been rediscovered by the Christian world shortly before St Thomas reached his intellectual height. Aquinas' most famous work is *Summa Theologica*, an exhaustive theological textbook in the form of questions and objections, answers and responses. Aquinas poses and answers a long series of questions about the nature of God, the Church and the sacramental system, while anticipating and responding to objections. It remains a hugely important resource for theology to this day.

For our purposes there is one feature of St Thomas' thought that bears particular mention.[27] As St Thomas applies his Aristotelian philosophical framework theologically, he develops a particular understanding of the nature of justice and rights.

Exactly what justice is remains a matter of debate even within contemporary philosophy. For Aquinas, justice has a peculiar meaning that might not immediately chime with our understanding of justice as fairness or diligent application of national or international law.

Instead for Aquinas, justice is a kind of relationship. This relationship engenders certain rights based on preserving this right relationship. As a human being I have certain rights to expect to be in right relationship with those people and things around me. If I'm torn out of that relationship through the sinful acts of others, it's my right to expect to be allowed back into right relationship, or to be put back into right relationship if it's outside of my capability.

Herbert McCabe puts this simply: 'Justice, for Aquinas is the stable disposition to give everyone his or her due; it is concerned with maintaining an equality between people . . . Justice, then, is essentiality about a relation to another and its criteria are objective.'[28]

Within his discussion of justice, Aquinas distinguishes between two kinds of justice: commutative and distributive.[29] Commutative has to do with justice between individuals, while distributive justice concerns what an individual can expect with regards to justice from society as a whole and as part of the Common Good. It is this distributive kind of justice with which Catholic Social Teaching is primarily concerned as it focuses on the rights of an individual in relation to the society as a whole – what an individual can justly expect from society, and the right ordering and relationships that need to exist within that society for justice to be obtained.

The 'right' of this kind of justice is derived from a kind of metaphysical basis that human beings have simply in virtue of their being human. Aquinas describes distributive justice as 'the order of the whole towards the parts, to which corresponds the order of that which belongs to the community in relation to each single person'.[30]

There is a lot of debate as to whether Aquinas' notion of rights (in Latin: *ius*) is the same as the notions of 'human' or 'universal' rights with which we are familiar today. John Finnis has concluded that they amount to the same, because of Aquinas' notion of justice, 'that *ius* belongs to those others whom you would injure if you violated the commandment, and who, accordingly, simply by being human beings, are entitled – it is their right – not to be so injured'.[31]

Modern notions of 'human rights' claim to be based on universality and humanity, but in truth they are upheld by a particular system of national and international law which has decided to uphold such rights. In contrast, 'rights' within Aquinas' thought have a metaphysical basis from the ordering and creation of the world by God. As McCabe notes, 'it is not at all clear that "human rights" as currently understood can make any sense if deprived of this metaphysical foundation . . . the only way an atheist could make sense of human rights is to see them as a development of positive international law, established by agreement between nations'.[32]

Thomist notions of 'rights' therefore do share the same metaphysical basis with the legal 'human rights' which currently, and we hope permanently, enjoy international agreement. According to Aquinas you enjoy 'rights' as a human being simply *because* you are a human being. Strictly speaking, in the modern world we enjoy 'human rights' because they are currently enforced by law. Should the law or the political class stop or change our understanding of those rights we may no longer enjoy those same 'human rights'. The important point is that within Thomist thought these rights do not change according to the whim of the legislators. They are ours simply by virtue of our humanity.

How does this relate to Catholic Social Teaching? We have already seen Cardinal Manning's appeal to 'natural law' to speak against the consequences of industrialization which have upset the proper ordering and balance of domestic life.[33] We see now how this appeal to natural law also sits within this Thomist tradition.

Even more pertinently for the development of Catholic Social Thought is the first social encyclical, *Rerum Novarum*, written by Pope Leo XIII in 1891. There we see him applying this Thomist notion of rights to the question of the appropriate level of pay in terms of wages, as we shall see below. He argues that human beings have a 'natural right to procure what is required in order to live, and the poor can procure that in no other way than by what they can earn through their work'.[34] Further, he notes that it is 'a dictate of natural justice that wages ought not to be insufficient to support a frugal and well-behaved wage-earner'.[35]

In this foundational document of Catholic Social Teaching, we see how that teaching relies heavily on a Thomas theological framework.

Rerum Novarum is written in response to the social problems caused by the divisions in society which arose through rapid industrialization, often setting rich against poor in the struggle for control of these new resources. Such divides had led to the birth of philosophies and ideologies which Pope Leo saw as threatening and potentially harmful to society. Pope Leo had earlier written of the possibilities that Thomist thought offered to bridge these newly opened divides, and to overcome the rise of ideologies which may have been damaging to the very people who held to them. He wrote in 1879: 'Domestic and civil society even, which, as all see, is exposed to great danger from this plague of perverse opinions, would certainly enjoy a far more peaceful and secure existence if a more wholesome doctrine were taught in the universities and high schools – one more in conformity with the teaching of the Church, such as is contained in the works of Thomas Aquinas.'[36]

The doctrine found in the teaching of Thomas Aquinas repeatedly lies behind much of what we shall read and explore below. Pope Leo's own encyclical would help introduce the world to that 'more wholesome doctrine' which speaks of justice for every human being, simply because of their humanity.

Dorothy Day (1897–1980)

Dorothy Day is famous for her association with the *Catholic Worker* newspaper and the network of 'Houses of Hospitality' which she founded and inspired across North America. These houses are still in existence today as places which seek to live out her vision for a practical application of Catholic Social Teaching.[37] She stands as an inspiration for all those who wish to live out the social justice at which that teaching aims. She calls us to 'just take the Gospels, a newspaper, the Papal encyclicals and get to work'.[38]

Throughout her life, in word and deed, the importance of the life and witness of Dorothy Day is apparent for those who wish to learn how to apply the insights of Catholic Social Teaching in their life and ministry. She stands as 'another expression, albeit an unusual and fervent one, of the great mainstream tradition of Catholic social thought that began with *Rerum Novarum*'.[39]

From an Anglican Episcopalian background, she wrote of her conversion through communist social action to Catholicism and Catholic social action in numerous publications. In 1938, an account of her conversion was published in the form of an apology addressed to her communist brother, *From Union Square to Rome*, which she expanded later into her famous autobiography, *The Long Loneliness*.[40]

Day writes of her conversion to belief in God through her work with and among the poor and alongside fellow communists: 'I found Him through His poor, and in a moment of joy turned to Him. I have said, sometimes flippantly, that the mass of bourgeois smug Christians who denied Christ in His poor made me turn to Communism, and that it was the Communists and working with them that made me turn to God.'[41]

A key moment in her conversion was her time in prison in 1917 as a result of activity in support of women's suffrage. She was sentenced to 30 days imprisonment along with others involved in the campaign and began a hunger strike. During this time she asked for a Bible, and she read it, especially the Psalms, 'with the sense of coming back to something of my childhood that I had lost . . . I read and pondered. Yet all the while I read, my pride was fighting on. I did not want to go to God in defeat and sorrow. I did not want to depend on Him. I was like the child that wants to walk by itself, I kept brushing away the hand that held me up. I tried to persuade myself that I was reading for literary enjoyment. But the words kept echoing in my heart. I prayed and did not know I prayed.'[42]

It would be a decade, and the birth of her only daughter Tamar Teresa in 1926, before Dorothy Day would ultimately turn back to God and his Church. Her desire for her child to be baptized led in turn to her Confirmation in the Roman Catholic Church: 'I knew that I was not going to have her floundering through many years as I had done . . . I felt it was the greatest thing I could do for a child. For myself, I prayed for the gift of faith. I was sure, yet not sure.'[43]

The significance of her child's birth in her journey to an active faith is obvious, as it provides the climax of her account in *From Union Square*. For our purposes, it's also important to note that the doctrine of the Mystical Body of Christ also takes a prominent place in that account. This is the doctrine that as members of the Church, Christians are members of one another as we are each members of Christ's body. We will encounter this doctrine below in Chapter 4 as we consider the principle of solidarity within Catholic Social Teaching.[44]

Day writes of her lessons in solidarity from within social activism which led her to understand the doctrine of the Mystical Body: 'All the nation, that is the poor, the worker, the trade unionist – those who felt most keenly the sense of solidarity – that very sense of solidarity which made me gradually understand the doctrine of the Mystical Body of Christ whereby we are the members of one another.'[45]

Once she came to realize her membership of that Body within the Roman Catholic Church, it took her some time to reconcile her faith with her sense of social concern. In 1932, on the feast of the Immaculate Conception, she prayed 'a special prayer, a prayer which came with tears and anguish, that some way God would open up for me to use what talents I possessed for my fellow workers, for the poor'.[46]

Returning home to New York, she met Peter Maurin – a man she would later describe as 'Apostle to the World'.[47] If the significance of her daughter's birth is shown by the role it plays in *From Union Square*, the significance of Peter Maurin is shown by his influence within *The Long Loneliness*. Day herself notes, having described their initial encounter, that his 'spirit and ideas will dominate the rest of this book as they will dominate the rest of my life'.[48] Peter Maurin was a campaigner for social justice who had initially lapsed from his Catholic faith, only to come to see that this faith was essential to bring about the social transformation for which he longed.

Maurin's aim was 'to make the encyclicals [of Catholic Social Teaching] click' for those around him.[49] It was Maurin's vision of a lively periodical to allow the message of Catholic Social Thought to reach a new audience, and 'houses of hospitality' to minister to the practical needs of that audience, which answered Dorothy Day's prayer for a means by which to unite her faith and sense of social justice and marked the rest of her career. When he died in 1949, Dorothy Day would continue their work for the rest of her life.

The first issue of the *Catholic Worker* was published in New York on 1 May 1933, shortly after their first meeting, and at the height of the Great Depression. The date is significant, both because 1 May had been commemorated as a day of international solidarity for all working people since the turn of the century, but also the very next day trade unionism would be banned in Nazi Germany. The events which would mark the course of the twentieth century were set in train.

Maurin's blank verse 'easy essays' on political subjects of the day became a feature of the periodical, and in the first edition he writes: 'The high ethics of the Canon Law are embodied in the encyclicals of Pius XI and Leo XIII on the social problem. To apply the ethics of the encyclicals to the problems of the day is the purpose of Catholic Action.'[50] Here we see what he meant by 'making the encyclicals click'. Day would later describe how this was achieved, in the face of those who wrote them off as hopeless communists or socialists: 'Nobody seems to understand that when we are out at strike meetings or picket lines or demonstrations distributing the paper, we are trying to bring the social teachings of the Church to the man in the street.'[51]

If Maurin had the vision of how to combine Catholic faith with social action, and make the encyclicals of Catholic Social Teaching 'click', it was Day who supplied the detail. She suggested the title *Catholic Worker* and provided the direction and energy to live out Maurin's vision: 'To change the hearts and minds of men . . . to give them vision – the vision of a society where it is easier for men to be good.'[52]

Following the first edition of the *Catholic Worker*, the circulation grew from 2,500 to 190,000 by 1938. Day soon developed the *Catholic Worker* into a network of action, centred on 'Houses of Hospitality', of which there are now over 200 worldwide.[53] Under Maurin and Day's inspiration these communities were homes trying to live according to the image of the early Church in Acts where all 'who believed were together and had all things in common; they would sell their possessions and goods and distribute the proceeds to all, as any had need' (Acts 2.44–45). These were places of voluntary poverty and common life, 'not a new philosophy but a very old philosophy, a philosophy so old that it looks like new'.[54]

'Houses of Hospitality' were needed, wrote Maurin, 'to give to the rich the opportunity to serve the poor. We need Houses of Hospitality to bring the Bishops to the people and the people to the Bishops. We need Houses of Hospitality to bring back to institutions the technique of institutions. We need Houses of Hospitality to show what idealism looks like when it is practiced.'[55] The nature of an institution will be important for us to bear in mind as we consider the principle of subsidiarity below. Likewise, we see here in concrete form notions within Catholic Social Teaching, of an 'option for the poor' and the inalienable dignity of every human person, being lived out.

Maurin's vision subverts the usual relation between rich and poor. The poor are not recipients of charity, but provide the rich an opportunity to serve. As Mel Piehl notes, 'the Catholic Workers insisted that they were not performing acts of charity or social service, but engaging in a "personalist revolution" by giving proper treatment to people who were, in the eyes of God, fully the equals of those who served them . . . It was actually the poor as "ambassadors of God", who were doing the favour.'[56] Maurin writes: 'We read in the Gospel: "As long as you did it to one of the least of my brothers, you did it to me." While modern society calls the beggars bums and panhandlers, they are in fact the Ambassadors of God. To be God's Ambassador is something to be proud of.'[57] The poor are reminded of a particular closeness with Christ which avoids the cycles of charity and service provision, achieving a pride which aims to restore that dignity which is an inalienable part of human personhood according to Catholic Social Teaching.

Shortly before she died, while appealing for funds to support the Catholic Worker project, Day reflected on the nature of the work to which she had committed her adult life: 'Sometimes, I think the purpose of the Catholic Worker, quite aside from our social aims, is to show the providence of God, how God loves. We are a family, not an institution, in atmosphere . . . This work came about because we started writing of the love we should have for each other, in order to show our love of God. It's the only way we can know we love God.'[58]

The witness of Dorothy Day gives us one example of a life which sought to make the great encyclicals of Catholic Social Teaching 'click'. As Sabrina Marsh has noted: 'For Day, articulating a faithful but radical translation of Catholic social teachings meant arguing for the relevance of papal texts at a time when American Catholics remained mostly unaware of the Church hierarchy's expressed mission.'[59] Day's life gives us one example of how to put Catholic Social Teaching into practice. Her legacy also reminds us of the importance of making that teaching known to as wide an audience in the world as possible in order to transform that world. To that task, we now turn.

Notes

1 International Commission on English in the Liturgy, *Roman Missal* (London: Catholic Truth Society, 2011), Preface II of the Saints', 634.

2 For the life of Mgr Jack Egan, see Frisbie, M., *An Alley In Chicago: The Life and Legacy of Monsignor John Egan* (Franklin: Sheed & Ward, 2002). We will encounter the discipline of community organizing throughout this book as an example of how to live out the principles of Catholic Social Teaching in everyday life. For an introduction to community organizing, see Bolton, M., *How to Resist* (London: Bloomsbury, 2017). For an example of how the principles of Catholic Social Teaching find an outworking in the practice of community organizing, see Ivereigh, A., *Faithful Citizens: A Practical Guide to Catholic Social Teaching and Community Organising* (London: Dartman, Longman & Todd, 2010).

3 Manning, H. E., *The Dignity and Rights of Labour* (London: Burns and Oates, 1874).

4 Manning, *Dignity.*

5 Smith, H. L. and Nash, V., *The Story of the Dockers' Strike* (London, 1889); also in Strachey, L., *Eminent Victorians* (London: Continuum, 2002), 102.

6 Tillett, B., *Memories and Reflections* (London: John Long, 1931).

7 *The Morning Post* (Issue 36579), 11 September 1889, 5.

8 Barry, W., 'Joy in Harvest', in Bourne, F. (ed.), *Catholic Emancipation 1829 to 1929* (Longmans, 1929), 12.

9 Cardijn, J. cited in De La Bedoyere, M., *The Cardijn Story* (London: Longmans, Green and Co, 1958), 12.

10 Cardijn in De La Bedoyere, *Cardijn*, 13.

11 Quoted in Arbuthnott, E., *Joseph Cardijn: Priest and Founder of the YCW* (London: Dartman, Longman & Todd, 1966), 11.

12 Cardijn, J., 'Worker Organisation in England', in *Revue Social Catholique* (Nov.–Dec. 1911), available in translation at: http://www.josephcardijn.com/worker-organisation-in-england (accessed 21 August 2018).

13 Cardijn, 'Worker Organisation'.

14 Arbuthnott, *Cardijn*, 11.

15 See De La Bedoyere, *Cardijn*, 42–45. For the later development of JOCF, an organization for young French women in working communities inspired by Cardijn's work, see Newsome, W., 'French Catholics, Women, and the Home: The Founding Generation of the Jeunesse ouvrière chrétienne féminine', in *Historical Reflections / Réflexions Historiques* 37.1 (Spring 2011), 18–44. She notes how, while JOCF primarily ascribes traditional roles to women of wife and mother, the application of the 'see-judge-act' method was an important means of intellectual development for JOCF members.

16 De La Bedoyere, *Cardijn*, 77.

17 Cardijn, J., 'Jeunesse Syndicaliste' (1920) in De La Bedoyere, *Cardijn*, 61.

18 De La Bedoyere, *Cardijn*, 78.

19 De La Bedoyere, *Cardijn*, 67.

20 For their growth in North America, see Zotti, M., 'The Young Christian Workers' in *U. S. Catholic Historian* 9.4 (1990), 387–400. More information on their work today can be found at: www.joci.org (accessed 21 August 2018).

21 Arnould, E. cited in Zotti, 'Young Christian Workers', 399.

22 *Quadragesimo*, 141.

23 *Quadragesimo*, 142.

24 Cardijn in De La Bedoyere, *Cardijn*, 81.

25 Cardijn in De La Bedoyere, *Cardijn*, 49.

26 There is a wide literature available on Aquinas, of which McCabe, H., *On Aquinas* (London: Continuum, 2008) is one of the most accessible. The first chapter offers a short biographical sketch of St Thomas.

27 The following section is put very simply, and oversimplifies a very large field of scholarship. For a more sophisticated treatment see Davies, B., *The Thought of Thomas Aquinas* (Oxford: Clarendon Press, 1992)

and Finnis, J. *Aquinas: Moral, Political and Legal Theory* (Oxford: Oxford University Press 1998).

28 McCabe, *On Aquinas*, 150.

29 *Summa Theologica* 2.2.61.

30 *Summa Theologica* 2.2.61, Article 1.

31 Finnis, J., 'Aquinas on *ius* and Hart on Rights: A Response to Tierney' in *The Review of Politics* 64.3 (Summer 2002), 407–10. Finnis earlier held an opposing view; see his *Natural Law and Natural Rights* (Oxford: Oxford University Press, 1980).

32 McCabe, *On Aquinas*, 156.

33 Manning, *Dignity*.

34 *Rerum*, 44.

35 *Rerum*, 45.

36 Aeterni Patris (1879), available at: http://w2.vatican.va/content/leo-xiii/en/encyclicals/documents/hf_l-xiii_enc_04081879_aeterni-patris.html (accessed 20 August 2018).

37 See www.catholicworker.org (accessed 4 July 2018) for more information about these houses today.

38 Day, D., 'Day after Day' in *Catholic Worker* (1 January 1939), 4.

39 Piehl, M., *Breaking Bread: The* Catholic Worker *and the Origin of Catholic Radicalism in America* (Tuscaloosa, AL: University of Alabama Press, 2006), 253.

40 Day, D., *From Union Square to Rome* (Preservation of the Faith Press, 1938) (reprinted Maryknoll, NY: Orbis Books, 2006); Day, D. *The Long Loneliness* (New York: Harper & Brothers, 1952).

41 Day, *Union Square*, 12.

42 Day, *Loneliness*, 80–1.

43 Day, *Union Square*, 131.

44 Frisbie, *Alley*, chapters 3 and 4, both for a brief account of wider Catholic America at this time and for the importance of the outworking of the Mystical Body of Christ as a doctrine for those in Catholic social action.

45 Day, *Union Square*, 144–5.

46 Day, *Loneliness*, 166.

47 Day, D., *Peter Maurin: Apostle to the World* (Maryknoll, NY: Orbis Books, 2004).

48 Day, *Loneliness*, 166.

49 Day, *Loneliness*, 194; Day, *Maurin*, 43.

50 Maurin, P., 'Ethics and Economics' in *Catholic Worker* 1.1 (1 May 1933). The encyclicals Maurin refers to are *Rerum Novarum*, published by Pope Leo XII, which we have already encountered and will encounter again below, and *Quadragesimo Anno*, written by Pius XI, and published on the fortieth anniversary of *Rerum Novarum*, which sees the beginning of *Rerum Novarum's* foundational status for Catholic Social Teaching.

51 Day, D., 'Day after Day' in *Catholic Worker* (1 January 1939), 4.

52 Day, *Loneliness*, 181.

53 Dorothy Day's own account of life in these houses of hospitality in New York was published as Day, D., *House of Hospitality* (London: Sheed & Ward, 1939).

54 Maurin, P., *The Green Revolution* (New York: Academy Guild Press, 1961), 76–7.

55 Maurin, P., 'Houses of Hospitality' in Day, *House of Hospitality*, xxiii.

56 Piehl, *Breaking Bread*, 103.

57 Cornell, T. and Forest, J., *A Penny a Copy* (New York: Macmillan, 1968), 17–18, cited in Piehl, *Breaking Bread*, 103.

58 Day, D., 'Fall Appeal 1977' in Ellsberg, R. (ed.), *Little by Little: The Selected Writings of Dorothy Day* (New York: A. A. Knopf, 1983), 358–9.

59 Marsh, S., '"The Odds and Ends of Things": Dorothy Day's 1930s *Catholic Worker* Columns and the Prudent Translation of Catholic Social Teachings' in *Rhetoric Society Quarterly* 42.4 (2012), 330–52, 331.

2

Personal Dignity

> The foundation of this teaching is the dignity of the human person. In virtue simply of our shared humanity, we must surely respect and honour one another. Each individual has a value that can never be lost and must never be ignored . . . The Church has the right and the duty to advocate a social order in which the human dignity of all is fostered, and to protest when it is in any way threatened.[1]
>
> *Cardinal Basil Hume*

The first principle of Catholic Social Teaching we will explore is the inalienable dignity of humankind.[2] We do so both because it is the first set out in the *Compendium of Social Doctrine of the Church*, and because it is the foundation of Catholic Social Thought, from which all of the other principles flow. It is fundamental to Catholic thought: 'On this basic principle, which guarantees the sacred dignity of the individual, the Church constructs her social teaching.'[3]

From the outset it's important to recognize that this notion of dignity is an outworking of the same principle which gives rise to more notorious aspects of the moral teaching of the Catholic Church. Pope Francis describes this difficulty: 'We find it difficult to make people see that when we raise other questions less palatable to public opinion, we are doing so out of fidelity to precisely the same convictions about human dignity and the Common Good.'[4]

We can give one such example – the Church's prohibition on abortion and teaching on marriage. The Second Vatican Council set out how these are related to the principle of human dignity:

'Whatever is opposed to life itself, such as any type of murder, genocide, abortion, euthanasia or wilful self-destruction, whatever violates the integrity of the human person, such as mutilation, torments inflicted on body or mind, attempts to coerce the will itself; whatever insults human dignity, such as subhuman living conditions, arbitrary imprisonment, deportation, slavery, prostitution, the selling of women and children; as well as disgraceful working conditions, where men are treated as mere tools for profit, rather than as free and responsible persons; all these things and others of their like are infamies indeed.'[5]

We see here that a whole range of activities are classed as 'infamies' if they violate the dignity of the human person. These range from social evils more usually associated with Catholic Social Teaching – the quality of homes to the treatment of individuals at work – to those acts which are identified as moral evils by the Catholic Church. It is not the place here to discuss the precise list of activities which the Catholic Church has discerned violate the inalienable dignity of the human person. For our purposes, we can see that both moral and social teaching stem from this same foundation – the belief in the inalienable dignity of humankind. It is this foundation which is the subject of this chapter.

This helps us see that Catholic Social Teaching is not an obscure part of Catholic thought, or the preserve of the political left or socially liberal. It is part and parcel of Catholic thought, as much as those aspects of Roman Catholic thought which might appeal more readily to those who are more socially or politically conservative. Catholic Social Teaching transcends political labels and groupings. Justin Welby has already reminded us that this teaching is an 'applied outworking of the good news of Jesus Christ in terms of social structures and social justice'.[6] As such, because it flows out of reflection on the Gospel, Catholic Social Teaching will be a challenge to each and every political formulation, because the Gospel is a challenge to each and every political formulation!

This chapter explores how the principle of the inalienable dignity of the human person flows from the Gospel itself. We explore the scriptural basis of this principle, before seeing how this is reflected and developed in the documents in which Catholic Social Teaching is found. Throughout, we will see how this principle which is fundamental to Catholic Social Thought also generates Catholic moral life and thought more generally. Finally, we explore the practical outworking of this principle. We will explore the challenge posed by recognizing the inalienable dignity of humankind as foundational for how we live as Christian communities. Finally, we explore how it might challenge the way we order and structure ourselves as Church.

Scriptural Basis

There are two scriptural bases from which the principle of the inalienable dignity of humankind is derived. The first is anthropological – it is based on something about the nature of humankind. The second is related but Christological – it is based on something to do with the nature of Christ. The result of both is that each and every human possesses a dignity which Catholic Social Teaching regards as always wrong to mar or destroy.

The anthropological basis is the creation of humankind in the image of God. We find this at the very beginning of the Bible, in the poetic account of creation given to us in the book of Genesis: 'Then God said, "Let us make humankind in our image, according to our likeness; and let them have dominion over the fish of the sea, and over the birds of the air, and over the cattle, and over all the wild animals of the earth, and over every creeping thing that creeps upon the earth." So God created humankind in his image, in the image of God he created them' (Gen. 1.26–27). So the Catechism notes that 'the dignity of the human person is rooted in his creation in the image and likeness of God'.[7]

Catholic Social Teaching therefore condemns anything which prevents individual human beings realizing the potential of the image of God within them. This means that it is the duty of the Christian to work for those conditions which allow other human beings to remain free to realize this image. In *Gaudium et Spes*, the Fathers of the Second Vatican Council explored how this freedom relates to the divine image: 'Authentic freedom is an exceptional sign of the divine image within man . . . Hence man's dignity demands that he act according to a knowing and free choice that is personally motivated and prompted from within, not under blind internal impulse nor by mere external pressure.'[8]

With such freedom as a goal in mind, Catholic Social Teaching envisages a human society ordered in such a way as to enable individuals to overcome constraints on freedom which come from being enslaved to internal impulses such as lust or greed. It also calls for such structures as might liberate individuals and communities from the external pressures of poverty or exploitation, as we shall see repeatedly in what follows.

The anthropological basis provides a list of activities which are to be condemned or overcome that put constraints on the image of God, such as killing, or making a fellow human suffer intolerable pain or deprivation. It might therefore be thought of as a negative principle. However, the Christological basis for the inalienable dignity of every person provides us with a list of positive activities that safeguard the dignity of every human person.

Humankind's creation in the image of God is the basis of the inalienable right to dignity. It is confirmed Christologically. Not only does God create us in his image, but recalls us to that image in Christ. The Catechism reminds us that 'it is in Christ, Redeemer and Saviour, that the divine image, disfigured in man by the first sin, has been restored to its original beauty and ennobled by the grace of God'.[9]

We also see how this dignity is recognized and enhanced by Christ's saving work in Pope John XXIII's encyclical *Pacem in Terris*: 'When, furthermore, we consider man's personal dignity from the standpoint of divine revelation, inevitably our estimate of it is incomparably increased. Men have been ransomed by the blood of Jesus Christ. Grace has made them sons and friends of God, and heirs to eternal glory.'[10] Likewise, John Paul II writes in *Evangelium Vitae* how this status conferred on humankind in Christ is found in every human being: 'In every child which is born and in every person who lives or dies we see the image of God's glory. We celebrate this glory in every human being, a sign of the living God, an icon of Jesus Christ.'[11]

This means that we are not only called to act towards our fellow human beings in certain ways because they too are created in God's image, but because they share with us in the humanity which Christ has redeemed and restored. John Paul II again underlines this: 'The Gospel of God's love for man, the Gospel of the dignity of the person and the Gospel of life are a single and indivisible Gospel.'[12] We are invited to look at humankind through God's eyes and to see how his being born and dying as one of us demonstrates how preciously he regards each and every single member of humankind: 'By contemplating the precious blood of Christ, the sign of his self-giving love, the believer learns to recognize and appreciate the almost divine dignity of every human being and can exclaim with ever renewed and grateful wonder: "How precious must man be in the eyes of the Creator, if he gained so great a Redeemer?" (from the Exsultet of the Easter Vigil).'[13]

This is the second scriptural basis for the principle of inalienable dignity. We each have an inalienable dignity because each of us shares our humanity with Christ, and if our humanity is marred it is as if that action is against Christ himself.[14] As we read in Matthew's Gospel, 'Just as you did it to one of the least of these who are members of my family, you did it to me' (Matt. 25.40).

This Christological basis, rooted in the logic of the incarnation and expanded upon in this parable of judgement from Matthew's Gospel, provides us with a positive list of actions by which the dignity of humankind is maintained. These are to feed the hungry, quench the thirst of the thirsty, welcome the stranger, clothe the naked, care for the sick, visit the prisoner. Along with burying the dead these are sometimes known as the 'corporal works of mercy'. They give an example of the positive action commended by the principle of inalienable dignity of humankind. They are not exhaustive as a list. They remind us that wherever a human being's dignity is being violated through a want or need it is in the power of another human being to meet or lessen, we have a duty to restore dignity to that person through positive action such as visiting the sick or alleviating hunger at whatever level we are able to act.

The remainder of this chapter explores how and where this principle appears in Catholic Social Teaching. We look at how and in what other ways the principle of the inviolable dignity of humankind features in Catholic Social Teaching, and how this might be safeguarded and lived out in the lives of Christian communities and churches.

Inalienable Dignity: A Recent Example

A recent example helps us to see what it might mean practically to reflect the inalienable dignity of the human person in our life and thought. It also demonstrates just how radical it might be to recognize the dignity of all human persons in such a way that that dignity really is *inalienable*.

Pope Francis has recently revised the *Catechism of the Catholic Church* (the volume which is the yardstick of Catholic doctrine). He has done so to clarify the Church's teaching on the death penalty. The Catechism had previously permitted the death penalty 'if this is the only possible way of effectively defending human lives against the unjust aggressor'.[15] It included a number of caveats which made clear that the Church was against the use of the death penalty in all but the most unavoidable circumstances. For example, 'if non-lethal means are sufficient to defend and protect people's safety from the aggressor' the death penalty would not be permissible. It viewed cases where the death penalty would be appropriate as 'very rare, if not practically nonexistent'. Other forms of punishment were nearly always to be preferred 'as more in conformity to the dignity of the human person'.

Pope Francis' revision is as a result of reflection on the extent of the dignity which belongs to all human beings. He notes: 'The dignity of the person is not lost even after the commission of very serious crimes.'[16] In doing so, he makes use of a line of reasoning which is found in earlier Catholic Social Teaching. Pope John XXIII had previously asserted: 'A man who has fallen into error does not cease to be a man. He never forfeits his personal dignity; and that is something that must always be taken into account.'[17] Likewise, John Paul II: 'Not even a murderer loses his personal dignity, and God himself pledges to guarantee this.'[18]

Anna Rowlands has noted against a flurry of immediate negative reaction that Francis' clarification does not represent a novelty but 'a line of reflection that has been slowly gathering pace: a case for the Church to call on those who animate law to exercise restraint in the use of the arsenal of cruel powers the state has at its disposal'.[19] The role of the State in promoting or inhibiting the dignity of its members occurs frequently in Catholic Social Thought, as we shall see below.

The most significant result of this shift is the call to action to work against the death penalty globally. From a previous position of rejection of the death penalty in almost every case, the Church is now committed not only to a passive rejection of this means of punishment but to actively working 'with determination for its abolition worldwide'.

The revised teaching on the death penalty cites an earlier intervention by Pope Francis: 'The death penalty is inadmissible because it is an attack on the inviolability and dignity of the person.'[20] The death penalty violates the inviolable dignity which remains even in the guiltiest of sinners.

All of this shows the extent of this human dignity as the foundation for Catholic Social Teaching. The rejection of the death penalty offers just one concrete example of what it means to believe in the dignity of each and every human being, regardless of who they are or what they do. We're reminded that there is nothing we can do to lose or surrender this dignity.

Catholic Social Teaching is a response, in part, to the changing social conditions and problems experienced by the human family in the industrialized age. As social problems change, so Catholic Social Teaching is articulated afresh to more clearly address the problems of the present age. This helps us to see both the flexibility of Catholic Social Thought, and its Thomistic inheritance. Anna Rowlands describes a central feature of this tradition, 'the relationship between changeable means and unchanging ends . . . the changing material nature of our lives means we will of necessity deploy that unchanging truth in historically differentiated ways'.[21] The *Compendium of the Social Doctrine of the Church* describes this process as 'perennial truth penetrates and permeates new circumstances, indicating paths of justice and peace'.[22]

We can see this clearly in respect of human dignity. As the means by which human dignity is offended changes across the course of time, so Catholic Social Teaching points out new ways in which the inviolable dignity of every person must be protected and upheld. For example, John Paul II reflects on how new technology brings news ways to violate human dignity: 'Far from decreasing . . . with the new prospects opened up by scientific and technological progress there arise new forms of attacks on the dignity of the human being.'[23]

Here we see the dignity upheld as an 'unchangeable end', but the means by which Catholic Social Teaching articulates how it is to be upheld shifts as the social conditions demand. As Rowlands notes, 'this is not relativism but the upholding of an idea of objective order and natural law in the realm of the finite'.[24]

We will now go on to explore how this dignity emerges in the documents of Catholic Social Teaching, and how changing social conditions are highlighted as new places where human dignity is violated.

Human Dignity and the World of Work

The first Catholic Social encyclical came in response to the rapidly changing, and worsening, working conditions within the industrialized nations of the West at the end of the nineteenth century. Pope Leo XIII, writing in 1891, did so in part because of the perceived threat of socialism and other responses to industrialization that might have appealed to some of the Catholic faithful, and risked destabilizing the social order.

Throughout the encyclical, socialism as a philosophy is condemned: 'Socialism, community of goods, must be utterly rejected, since it only injures those whom it would seem meant to benefit, is directly contrary to the natural rights of mankind, and would introduce confusion and disorder into the commonweal.'[25] We shall look at Pope Leo's defence of private property as a natural right and human good in the following chapter. As we focus on the principle of human dignity, Pope Leo draws attention to the violations of dignity occurring in the world of work at the time, and offers a set of recommendations for Catholic employers and employees to safeguard the dignity of the human person.

The encyclical opens by reflecting on the 'misery and wretchedness pressing so unjustly on the majority of the working class . . . a small number of very rich men have been able to lay upon the teeming masses of the labouring poor a yoke little better than that of slavery itself'.[26] While Pope Leo doesn't directly connect this condition with the violation of human dignity, his successor Pius XI makes clear this link when reflecting on the influence of Pope Leo's encyclical 40 years later. Improvements in working conditions help to safeguard 'the sacred rights of workers that flow from their dignity as men and as Christians'.[27]

Pius XI reflected on the breadth of areas within the world of work which can safeguard or violate the dignity of the human worker: 'The protection of life, health, strength, family, homes, workshops, wages and labor hazards . . . everything which pertains to the condition of wage workers, with special concern for women and children'.[28] He notes how the nature of work must recognize 'the worker's human dignity . . . [and] therefore cannot be bought and sold like a commodity'.[29] Pope Benedict XVI recently reaffirmed this bold vision of the kind of work 'that expresses the essential dignity of every man and woman in the context of their particular society . . . work that leaves enough room for rediscovering one's roots at a personal, familial and spiritual level'.[30]

In *Rerum Novarum*, Pope Leo had pointed out ways that the world of work might respect and not violate the human dignity of the worker. These concern the conditions and place of work in the whole life of the worker, the rate of pay and the fellowship between workers in unions and associations. These associations we will explore in Chapter 5 as we consider the principle of subsidiarity. Stemming from *Rerum Novarum*, support for a living wage and just conditions in the workplace are two means by which Catholic Social Teaching has sought to safeguard the dignity of every human being.

Living Wage, Dignified Work

Support for a just or living wage has been a constant feature of Catholic Social Teaching. It is promoted in the belief that a just wage best safeguards the dignity of the employee. Poverty pay undermines the dignity of the worker, and so a worker should be paid enough to maintain the dignity that he or she has as a human being.

The basis for the Catholic support of this wage is therefore based on the dignity of the human person. The call for a just wage features in *Rerum Novarum*, and has been reiterated recently by Pope Francis: 'A just wage enables them to have adequate access to all the other goods which are destined for our common use.'[31]

The call for a living wage has its roots in Scripture. The phrase '[a] labourer deserves his wages' (Luke 10.7) is well known to the author of the first letter to Timothy (1 Tim. 5.18). In *Evangelii Gaudium*, Pope Francis points to James 5.4: 'The wages of the labourers who mowed your fields, which you kept back by fraud, cry out.'

Within Catholic Social Teaching, this support for a living wage to promote the human dignity of the worker also finds its basis in the Thomist tradition of rights. Leo XIII identifies such a wage as part of the 'natural right to procure what is required in order to live'.[32] Failure to do so, Leo writes, is a violation of 'a dictate of natural justice more imperious and ancient than any bargain between man and man, namely, that wages ought not to be insufficient to support a frugal and well-behaved wage-earner'.[33] Likewise, Pius XII writes: 'Nature imposes work upon man as a duty, and man has the corresponding natural right to demand that the work he does shall provide him with the means of livelihood for himself and his children. Such is nature's categorical imperative for the preservation of man.'[34] Theodor Herr describes the radical challenge of this notion of rights: 'Worker's rights belong, like social rights, to humanity's original rights and are, like them, inalienable and untouchable.'[35]

This appeal to natural law in defence of the right of the worker to demand fair pay is also found in the first book-length treatment of the subject. John Ryan, sometime Professor of Moral Theology at the Catholic University of America, echoes this rights-based argument in his 1906 book *Living Wage*.[36] He argued that failure to pay a living wage is an abuse of the worker's inviolable right of potential to human flourishing, and thus an assault on their inviolable dignity as a person.

The 'just wage' or 'living wage' is envisaged within Catholic Social Teaching as sufficient to support a family to a standard deemed minimally acceptable: 'The amount a worker receives must be sufficient, in proportion to available funds, to allow him and his family a standard of living consistent with human dignity.'[37]

It should be noted here that the concept of a living wage, based on the inviolable dignity of the person and their natural right to obtain such a wage, is contested by some Catholic commentators.[38] Many of these adhere to an economic theory outside of that found in the documents of Catholic Social thought. They argue that calls for a 'just wage' are short-sighted as wages are best determined by what the market can afford. If they are not, then the worker may end up without work or with less work and pay than before the payment of a just wage. The setting of wages is contested within economic theory, with others noting that minimum and higher wages increase productivity and levels of staff retention, and therefore reduce costs of training and recruitment.[39] Some arguments for keeping pay at low levels do so in order to benefit shareholders and company owners over low-paid employees, and thus constitute an example of the kind of violation of human dignity with which Catholic Social Teaching is concerned.

The inviolable dignity of the human being also means that Catholic Social Teaching is concerned not only with the rates of pay, but the quality and conditions of work. In *Mater et Magistra*, Pope John XXIII lays out a vision for this sort of work. The environment in which the workers work must not be such as 'may prove harmful to their material and spiritual interests'.[40] Daniel Finn suggests this goes beyond what agreement is made between an employer and individual worker: 'Fundamental respect for human dignity is required in justice in all labor contracts or they are simply unjust.'[41]

More positively, the conditions of work must be such as to maintain and inspire personal initiative. Initiative in the workplace is part of what drives productivity (which in Britain is famously low compared to similar countries), but also serves to promote and maintain the dignity of the individual. If a worker is allowed space to exercise personal initiative it will increase their sense of dignity and personal value. John XXIII writes against a workplace or economic system which 'lessens a man's sense of responsibility or robs him of opportunity for exercising personal initiative'.[42] This challenges those managing workforces to create workplaces which allow space for such initiative.

As to whose duty it is to ensure that such an environment is maintained, John XXIII highlights the role of the State 'to ensure that terms of employment are regulated in accordance with justice and equity, and to safeguard the human dignity of workers'.[43] The question of the respective role of the State, the individual, the employer, the employee, and so on, is part of the constant balancing act of competing interests, which is a feature of this body of thought. We will encounter it again below as we discuss the principle of subsidiarity, and discuss the appropriate level of responsibility, influence and decision-making across the layers of society.

While silent on the means by which the State might achieve this, John XXIII is clear elsewhere how this must not be done. No form of coercion can be used by the State in achievement of this, or any, end. Indeed, such compulsion would be at odds with the kind of free and personal initiative in the workplace which Catholic Social Teaching recognizes is demanded by the human dignity of workers. He writes that 'the appeal of rulers should be to the individual conscience, to the duty which every man has of voluntarily contributing to the Common Good. But since all men are equal in natural dignity, no man has the capacity to force internal compliance on another. Only God can do that, for He alone scrutinizes and judges the secret counsels of the heart.'[44] This appeal to the good nature of the individual may strike us as naive. We might appeal to more positive means of encouragement to the employer or manager which suggest the benefits of recognizing the dignity of the worker for a productive and flourishing workplace in the long term.

Finally, Catholic Social Teaching insists that work must not be the only feature of the worker's life. For the worker to have their inviolable dignity recognized, recreation and rest must also feature: 'To safeguard man's dignity as a creature of God endowed with a soul in the image and likeness of God, the Church has always demanded a diligent observance of the third Commandment: "Remember that thou keep holy the sabbath day."'[45] This approach to the workplace, good pay, a healthy working environment, space for personal initiative and decent rest will help to contribute to a productive and flourishing economic system, which also safeguards the dignity of each and every worker.

If this vision of a workplace is bold, the overall thrust of the documents is simple. If the workplace and economic system do not prioritize the inviolable dignity of the worker as a human being then, whatever the fruits of that labour, they will ultimately come to nothing. Pope John XIII puts this in stark terms. The basic principle of Catholic Social Teaching is also the basic principle of the kind of work this teaching demands: 'individual human beings are the foundation, the cause and end of every social institution'.[46] Pope John Paul II underlines this in *Laborem Exercens*: 'Once more the fundamental principle must be repeated: the hierarchy of values and the profound meaning of work itself require that capital should be at the service of labour and not labour at the service of capital.'[47] If not, as John XXIII warns, 'there will be no peace nor justice in the world until they return to a sense of their dignity as creatures and sons of God, who is the first and final cause of all created being'.[48]

The vision of Catholic Social Teaching is for a system of employment in which each and every person is recognized as having the dignity which is theirs by right. In short, they must never be instrumentalized to serve some 'greater' end, whether profit or the pleasure or convenience of another.[49] Each human being in the chain of employment must be considered for what they 'are', not what they 'have, do, and produce'.[50]

What does such work look like? It might be that it requires a sea change in how we relate to cost and convenience. Artificially low-cost items whose price is achieved at the expense of the dignity of those who produce them might need to be removed from the marketplace. Likewise, convenience for the consumer which comes at the expense of the dignity of the employee might need to be rethought. If we live in such a way as to expect that deliveries can be made at all hours of the day and shops are open 24/7 at the expense of the rest and holiday of others, we may risk our wealth restricting the dignity of others.

In the West, this restriction of convenience might be an uncomfortable transition in a culture which has got used to seeing 'progress' as meaning longer opening hours and more 'convenient' forms of customer service. Humankind, not profit or convenience, must once again be 'the source, the centre, and the purpose of all economic and social life'.[51]

Dignity at Home

The vision for human dignity does not stop at the workplace. Catholic Social Teaching also recognizes the importance of living conditions which reflect the dignity of each person. Pope Francis notes that 'lack of housing is a grave problem in many parts of the world . . . Having a home has much to do with a sense of personal dignity and the growth of families.'[52]

In many countries housing is an increasing concern. House prices and rents are rising, conditions worsening, and the availability of good-quality housing stock close to places of work is diminishing. This restricts not only sleep and recreation, but lowers productivity at work and educational achievements of children within families. Not having a quiet, comfortable space for children to study and do homework at home can impact negatively on educational performance with consequences that can last decades.

The Archbishop of Canterbury, Justin Welby, has written from an Anglican perspective on the importance of housing. His *Reimagining Britain* is, as we have seen, in part an attempt to apply the principles of Catholic Social Teaching within an Anglican context to the problems facing contemporary Britain. He writes: 'If the purpose of housing was understood as creating communities and not merely building accommodation, the whole nature of the industry would be changed. The revolution would be even more profound if the incentive for housing was to have a good and safe shelter in a safe and convenient location, not principally an investment.'[53] In short, houses should be homes, not assets.

There are some innovative responses to the challenge to human dignity faced in the quality and availability of housing. Catholics and other Christians have been involved in the setting up of Community Land Trusts. Such trusts are properties bought by residents as a home, not an asset, to be sold on only at a rate linked to local earnings and not for profit.[54]

Housing is more than shelter. Paul VI highlights the role of housing in building the kind of community to which Justin Welby suggests housing should be oriented. Without proper community, people retreat behind facades of individual misery, Paul VI writes: 'Behind the facades much misery is hidden, unsuspected even by the closest neighbours; other forms of misery spread where human dignity founders.'[55] Well-planned and furnished housing fosters dignity not only by the standard of accommodation, but by its ability to foster community and relationship. Vincent Rougeau explains that 'the relationship between human dignity and human community is integral to a Catholic understanding of justice. Human persons are not seen as isolated individuals . . . but as members of communities and societies.'[56] Housing must not only foster the dignity of the individual, but allow that individual to take their place in the community in which they live if their dignity is truly to be recognized.

In terms of Catholic Social Teaching, the yardstick by which housing will be judged is the extent to which it reflects and safeguards the dignity of the occupant. Catholic Social Teaching calls on every society and community to ensure that each member of that society 'has everything necessary for leading a life truly human, such as food, clothing, and shelter'.[57]

Dignity and Our Common Home

Increasingly, Catholic Social Teaching has drawn attention not to the standard and treatment of earthly homes but the planet earth as 'our common home'.[58] This is the subtitle of an entire encyclical written by Pope Francis, *On Care for Our Common Home*.[59] While Pope Francis' contribution to the debate around environmental policy has drawn criticism from those suspicious of the observable threat of climate change, he builds on a theme previously found within the documents.

Pope Benedict wrote of the need to protect our common home for future generations: 'On this earth there is room for everyone . . . at the same time we must recognize our grave duty to hand the earth on to future generations in such a condition that they too can worthily inhabit it and continue to cultivate it.'[60] This vision is ground in the promotion of dignity: 'The entire human family must find the resources to live with dignity.'[61]

Pope Francis extends this line of thinking, criticizing 'the current global system where priority tends to be given to speculation and the pursuit of financial gain'.[62] In doing so, he links human dignity with our care for the natural environment. He does this both in respect of the impact of the current economic system, and the responsibility towards our natural environment that our dignity brings: 'By virtue of our unique dignity and our gift of intelligence, we are called to respect creation.'[63]

He expounds further on this obligation, including a care for our fellow creatures. He even goes so far as to suggest recycling is an expression of our inviolable dignity: 'Reusing something instead of immediately discarding it, when done for the right reasons, can be an act of love which expresses our own dignity.'[64]

The call to ecology is a means to safeguard the future dignity of the human beings that will follow us. It is therefore an expression of solidarity of the sort we shall explore in Chapter 4 below. Care for the planet is also an obligation arising out of dignity. To act carelessly or selfishly with respect to the planet, Pope Francis teaches, is to undermine or mar our dignity as those created in the image of the creator of heaven and earth.

Dignity and Femininity[65]

> If we are honest, we acknowledge that the fullness of women's participation in the church has not yet arrived . . . We have to work harder to develop a profound theology of women.

> I would add that an ecclesiology . . . that includes women is equally needed if women's roles are to be included as they should. Indeed, the inclusion of women in the Church is a creative way to promote the necessary changes in it. A theology and an ecclesiology of women should change the image, the concept and the structures of the Church.[66]

These words are those of Fr Arturo Sosa, Superior General of the Jesuits speaking at the 'Voices of Faith' conference. This conference has taken place at the Vatican on International Women's Day in recent years. Pope Francis likewise has noted that 'the firm conviction that men and women are equal in dignity, presents the Church with profound and challenging questions which cannot be lightly evaded'.[67]

He also notes that the restriction of the priesthood to males in the Roman Catholic Church, and the equation of ministerial power with power in general, 'can prove especially divisive'. He has consistently spoken and written elsewhere against such clericalism and identification of power 'which forgets that the visibility and sacramentality of the Church belong to all the People of God'.[68]

Partly because women do not exercise the ministerial priesthood with the Roman Catholic Church, many have noted it has not always been a place where the full dignity of women has been recognized. Simona Berretta, for example, points out 'that structures of power within the Church were and remain largely male; this can, and maybe should, be reformed'.[69] Most famously, Mary Daly applied the theory of the philosopher Simone de Beauvoir to the Roman Church in her *The Church and the Second Sex*.[70]

Pope Paul VI is representative of the Church's dismissal of what it deems 'false equality' of women while 'recognizing her independence as a person, and her equal rights to participate in cultural, economic, social and political life'.[71] All too often the documents of the Church speak about or to women as an object of discussion, rather than as people of equal dignity who have their own right as such to speak and be heard.

However, the documents which make up the body of Catholic Social Teaching are clear that the inviolable dignity of humankind means exactly that – the dignity of all humankind. *Pacem in Terris* reflects this most clearly: 'Women are gaining an increasing awareness of their natural dignity. Far from being content with a purely passive role or allowing themselves to be regarded as a kind of instrument, they are demanding both in domestic and in public life the rights and duties which belong to them as human persons.'[72]

The recognition of the full dignity of all human beings is the recognition of every human being, regardless of sex or gender. Likewise, this means there is no place for discrimination on the basis of race. John XXIII puts this most clearly: 'Truth calls for the elimination of every trace of racial discrimination.'[73] Every human being is simply valued as a human being, each created in God's image.

Dignity Lived Out

Finally, we come to consider what the inviolable right to dignity might mean in practical terms for those of us who seek to live and build Christian communities.

Catholic Social Teaching is not merely an analysis or description of social ailments and remedies. It is also a call to action. We find this emphasized from the very beginning of Catholic Social Teaching. Pope Leo XIII writes in *Rerum Novarum*: 'The Church, not content with pointing out the remedy, also applies it.'[74]

As we consider each of the principles of Catholic Social Teaching in this book, we will see how Christian communities might apply them, and what they might look like if they do so. This is especially the focus of Chapter 9.

Pope Francis suggests that failure to prioritize the principles of Catholic Social Teaching, especially the inviolability of human dignity, risks undermining the stability of any Christian community: 'Any Church community, if it thinks it can comfortably go its own way without creative concern and effective cooperation in helping the poor to live with dignity and reaching out to everyone, will also risk breaking down, however much it may talk about social issues or criticize governments.'[75] He goes further, adding that not to take such principles seriously, and act on them, risks 'a spiritual worldliness camouflaged by religious practices, unproductive meetings and empty talk'.[76] Actions speak louder than words.

This isn't to say that words don't have their place. A Christian community which takes human dignity seriously will not stop calling attention to other organizations which are acting in ways that mar or violate the dignity of any human being. As Pope Francis enjoins: 'When these values are threatened, a prophetic voice must be raised.'[77]

However, such a community will also never stop applying that voice to itself. A Christian community that is structured in such a way as to protect and promote the human dignity of each and every member will always be evaluating itself according to this principle. For example, we have seen how there are voices, within the Church, who recognize there is some way for the Church to go to take full account of the inviolable dignity of women as fellow human beings.

More practically, the standards which Catholic Social Teaching demands are in place to safeguard human dignity in the world of work and beyond will be in place within the Church. There can be no double standards. For example, where the Church is an employer she must be exemplary in paying just wages, caring for the environment, maintaining the work–life balance of employees, and so on.

In addition, volunteers should also be utilized in such a way as their dignity is promoted even while their skills and time are used in the service of the Church. The most obvious danger here is that any volunteer becomes an instrument of the wider programme or set of activities embarked upon by the Christian community. Instead, their dignity must always be borne in mind. Is their voluntary service contributing or detracting from their flourishing and dignity? Or is their labour and usefulness to the Church being valued above who they are in God's sight?

Building and maintaining such a community, experience teaches us, will not be easy. However, this does not mean that it should not be attempted. Our dignity demands it: 'No one can strip us of the dignity bestowed upon us by this boundless and unfailing love. With a tenderness which never disappoints, but is always capable of restoring our joy, he makes it possible for us to lift up our heads and to start anew. Let us not flee from the resurrection of Jesus, let us never give up, come what will. May nothing inspire more than his life, which impels us onwards!'[78]

Notes

1 Hume, B., 'Preface' in *The Common Good and the Catholic Church's Social Teaching* (London: Catholic Bishop's Conference of England and Wales, 1996), 1.

2 See also Herr, T., *Catholic Social Teaching: A Textbook of Christian Insights* (London: New City, 1991), 68 –72.

3 *Mater et Magistra* (Encyclical of Pope John XXIII on Christianity and Social Progress, 15 May 1961), 220, available at: http://w2.vatican.va/content/john-xxiii/en/encyclicals/documents/hf_j-xxiii_enc_15051961_mater.html (accessed 30 July 2018). See also *Pastoral Constitution on the Church in the Modern World Gaudium et Spes*, 40, available at: http://w2.vatican.va/content/john-paul-ii/en/encyclicals/documents/hf_jp-ii_enc_25031995_evangelium-vitae.html (accessed 30 July 2018): 'The dignity of the human person, and about the human community and the profound meaning of human activity, lays the foundation for the relationship between the Church and the world, and provides the basis for dialogue between them.'

4 *Evangelii Gaudium*, 65.

5 *Gaudium*, 27.

6 Welby, J., *Reimagining Britain: Foundations for Hope* (London: Bloomsbury, 2018), 35.

7 *Catechism*, 1700.

8 *Gaudium*, 17.

9 *Catechism*, 1701.

10 *Pacem*, 10.

11 *Evangelium Vitae*, 84.

12 *Evangelium Vitae*, 2.

13 *Evangelium Vitae*, 25.

14 *Gaudium*, 22: 'For by His incarnation the Son of God has united Himself in some fashion with every man.'

15 *Catechism of the Catholic Church*, 2267, available at: http://www.vatican.va/archive/ENG0015/_INDEX.HTM (accessed 3 August 2018).

16 'New revision of number 2267 of the Catechism of the Catholic Church on the death penalty – Rescriptum "ex Audentia SS.mi", 02.08.2018', available at: http://press.vatican.va/content/salastampa/en/bollettino/pubblico/2018/08/02/180802a.html (accessed 3 August 2018).

17 *Pacem in Terris* (Encyclical of Pope John XXIII on Establishing Universal Peace in Truth, Justice, Charity, and Liberty – April 11, 1963), 158, available at: http://w2.vatican.va/content/john-xxiii/en/encyclicals/documents/hf_j-xxiii_enc_11041963_pacem.html (accessed 30 July 2018). This section continues to supply a line of thought that recognizes another reason the death penalty violates human dignity is that it prevents the possibility of repentance to which all of us are called: 'Today, maybe, a man lacks faith and turns aside into error; tomorrow, perhaps, illumined by God's light, he may indeed embrace the truth.'

18 *Evangelium Vitae* (1995), 9, available at: http://w2.vatican.va/content/john-paul-ii/en/encyclicals/documents/hf_jp-ii_enc_25031995_evangelium-vitae.html (accessed 30 July 2018).

19 Rowlands, A., *Misunderstanding Francis: Catholic Social Teaching and the Death Penalty Debate*, available at: http://www.abc.net.au/religion/articles/2018/08/04/4879584.htm (accessed 6 August 2018).

20 Pope Francis, 'Address to Participants in the Meeting organized by the Pontifical Council for the Promotion of the New Evangelization, 11 October 2017', in *L'Osservatore Romano*, 13 October 2017, 5.

21 Rowlands, 'Misunderstanding Francis'.

22 *Compendium*, 86.

23 *Evangelium Vitae*, 4.

24 Rowlands, 'Misunderstanding Francis'.

25 *Rerum Novarum – Encyclical of Pope Leo XIII on Capital and Labour*, 15, available at: http://w2.vatican.va/content/leo-xiii/en/encyclicals/documents/hf_l-xiii_enc_15051891_rerum-novarum.html (accessed 30 July 2018).

26 *Rerum Novarum*, 3.

27 *Quadragesimo Anno*, 28, available at: http://w2.vatican.va/content/pius-xi/en/encyclicals/documents/hf_p-xi_enc_19310515_quadragesimo-anno.html (accessed 30 July 2018).

28 *Quadragesimo*, 28. See below on the question of dignity and housing.

29 *Quadragesimo*, 83.

30 *Caritas In Veritate*, available at: http://w2.vatican.va/content/benedict-xvi/en/encyclicals/documents/hf_ben-xvi_enc_20090629_caritas-in-veritate.html (accessed 1 May 2018), 63.

31 *Evangelii Gaudium*, 192.

32 *Rerum Novarum*, 44.

33 *Rerum Novarum*, 45.

34 Pius XII's broadcast message (1 June 1941), cited in *Pacem*, 20.

35 Herr, *Catholic Social Teaching*, 71.

36 Ryan, J. A., *A Living Wage: Its Ethical and Economic Aspects* (New York: Macmillan, 1906). See also Ryan, J. A., *Distributive Justice* (New York: Macmillan, 1916) and Brady, B. V., *Essential Catholic Social Thought* (New York: Maryknoll, 2008), 74–7.

37 *Pacem*, 20.

38 See especially, Booth, P., *Catholic Social Teaching and the Market Economy* (London: Institute of Economic Affairs and St Paul's Publishing, 2014). The text as a whole prioritizes a brand of free market economics over Catholic Social Teaching, while attempting to take account of those insights of Catholic Social Teaching which are followable within this economic system.

39 See for example www.livingwage.org.uk (accessed 3 August 2018).

40 *Mater*, 21.

41 Finn, D. K., 'The Unjust Contract: A Moral Evaluation' in Finn, D. K., *The True Wealth of Nations: Catholic Social Thought and Economic Life* (Oxford: Oxford University Press, 2010), 143–64, 149.

42 *Mater*, 83. See also *Pacem*, 34–5: 'Man's personal dignity requires besides that he enjoy freedom and be able to make up his own mind when he acts . . . human society thrives on freedom, namely, on the use of means which are consistent with the dignity of its individual members, who, being endowed with reason, assume responsibility for their own actions.'

43 *Mater*, 21.

44 *Pacem*, 48.

45 *Mater*, 249.

46 *Mater*, 219.

47 *Laborem*, 23.

48 *Mater*, 215.

49 See *Laborem*, 7: 'as an instrument and not in accordance with the true dignity of his work – that is to say, where he is not treated as subject and maker, and for this very reason as the true purpose of the whole process of production'.

50 *Evangelium Vitae*, 23; see also *Centesimus Annus*, available at: https://w2.vatican.va/content/john-paul-ii/en/encyclicals/documents/hf_jp-ii_enc_01051991_centesimus-annus.html (accessed 30 July 2018), 99.

51 *Gaudium*, 63.

52 *Evangelii Gaudium*, 152.

53 Welby, *Reimagining*, 128. For his argument for the need to reimagine housing, see 127–48.

54 For example, London's first in Mile End (http://www.londonclt.org) (accessed 30 July 2018). For other innovative approaches to the

problem of housing and community in a Latin American context, see McGuirk, J., *Radical Cities* (London: Verso, 2014).

55 *Octogesima Adveniens*, available at: http://w2.vatican.va/content/paul-vi/en/apost_letters/documents/hf_p-vi_apl_19710514_octogesima-adveniens.html (accessed 30 July 2018), 10.

56 Rougeau, V., 'Just Contracts and Catholic Social Teaching' in Finn, *Wealth*, 117–41.

57 *Gaudium*, 26.

58 See Pontifical Council for Justice and Peace, 'Chapter Ten: Safeguarding the Environment' in *Compendium of the Social Doctrine of the Church*, 228–45.

59 Laudato Si', On Care for Our Common Home, available at: http://w2.vatican.va/content/francesco/en/encyclicals/documents/papa-francesco_20150524_enciclica-laudato-si.html (accessed 30 July 2018).

60 *Caritas*, 50.

61 *Caritas*, 50.

62 *Laudato*, 56.

63 *Laudato*, 69.

64 *Laudato*, 211.

65 For the economic status of women as a means for testing the economic progress of society as a whole in the light of Catholic Social Teaching, see Beretta, S., 'What Do We Know about the Economic Status of Women, and What Does It Mean for a Just Economy?' in Finn (ed.), *Wealth*, 227–65.

66 Sosa, A., 'Stirring the Waters – Making the Impossible Possible' (Vatican, 8 March 2017), available at: https://www.xavier.edu/jesuit-resource/online-resources/documents/Sosa-MakingtheImpossiblePossibleAddressonWomen2.pdf (accessed 22 July 2018).

67 *Evangelii Gaudium*, 104.

68 Pope Francis, 'Letter of His Holiness Pope Francis to Cardinal Marc Ouellet, President of the Pontifical Commission for Latin America' (19 March 2016), available at: https://w2.vatican.va/content/francesco/en/letters/2016/documents/papa-francesco_20160319_pont-comm-america-latina.html (accessed 22 July 2018). The letter is a passionate attack on clericalism which should be read by every person exercising the ministerial priesthood. Beretta notes: 'the actual history of the Church, past and present, is driven by saints – men and women, married and consecrated to God, much more than by clerical (male) institutions!' ('Economic Situation', 253).

69 Beretta, 'Economic Situation', 253.

70 Daly, M., *The Church and the Second Sex* (London: Geoffrey Chapman Ltd, 1968). See Kennedy, P., *Twentieth Century Theologians: A New Introduction to Modern Christian Thought* (London: I. B. Tauris, 2010), 177–90; Bohache, T., *Christology from the Margins* (London: SCM Press, 2008), 106–14.

71 *Octogesima*, 13.
72 *Pacem*, 41.
73 *Pacem*, 86.
74 *Rerum*, 26.
75 *Evangelii Gaudium*, 207.
76 *Evangelii Gaudium*, 207.
77 *Evangelii Gaudium*, 218.
78 *Evangelii Gaudium*, 3.

3

Common Good

> As St. Ambrose put it: 'You are not making a gift of what is yours to the poor man, but you are giving him back what is his. You have been appropriating things that are meant to be for the common use of everyone. The earth belongs to everyone, not to the rich.'[1]

If the dignity of each human being is the principle which safeguards and promotes the rights of each person as an individual, the next principle of Catholic Social Teaching reminds us of what is held in common between all of us as humankind. The principle of 'the Common Good' is possibly the most diffuse of all the principles of Catholic Social Teaching.

There are two potentially conflicting understandings of 'good' within the body of Catholic Social Teaching, both of which are ascribed to common humanity or groups of people. The first is a moral 'Common Good' which is held to be for the good of all humankind, or at least all of the people in the community envisaged. This is occasionally referred to as the 'sum' of goods all individuals can expect to share in.

The second understanding of 'Common Good' is to do with the nature of 'goods' rather than moral 'good'. This relates to the question of property, and the extent to which property or 'goods' should be held in common. That is, whether they should be owned communally, or by the whole of humankind, or whether all goods should be used in such a way as to benefit the Common Good of all humankind each and every time they are used. This principle of Catholic Social Teaching therefore strikes at the heart of the tension between common ownership and private property which runs through the Christian tradition.

We shall see that Catholic Social Teaching rules out a casual dismissal of both the right to private property and also the common ownership of all things. However, this does not mean that the body of thought does not tend towards a particular understanding of how each and every good should be used for the good of all. We shall see how private property, insofar as it is held as a right within Catholic Social Teaching, is regarded as such only as a means of administration of each good which properly belongs to us and all, and, indeed, the whole of creation, or rather the Creator of every 'good' himself.

Scriptural Basis

In the book of Acts, we find an image of the Church which has been long disputed: 'All who believed were together and had all things in common; they would sell their possessions and goods and distribute the proceeds to all, as any had need' (Acts 2.44–45).

For many, this passage indicates an early form of Christian communism. They go on to infer that Christians should do likewise. The early Church held property in common, and so should we. Others suggest that there was never such a time or practice in the early Church. The image given in Acts is an ideal one, to present the harmony and unity of the early apostolic period.

A key gloss here occurs at the end of verse 45. They distributed the proceeds of the sale of possessions 'according to need'. This isn't communal ownership as a rule, but when need arises and another member of the community is lacking. One member of the community can't live with surplus, while the other lacks necessities.

However, and inconveniently for those who wish to maintain the passage in Acts 2 as an isolated instance of an idealized image, the author repeats this description and goes further. In Acts 4, we read how 'the whole group of those who believed were of one heart and soul, and no one claimed private ownership of any possessions, but everything they owned was held in common' (Acts 4.32). Here, not only is distribution also linked to need (Acts 4.35) but private ownership is eschewed.

Likewise, this theme can be traced in the early reception of these texts to suggest that ownership of property was directed towards the Common Good within at least some parts of the early Church, not simply as an ideal. Clement of Alexandria (*c.* 150–215 CE) instructs: 'God . . . made all things for all. All things therefore are common . . . For God has given us, I know well, the liberty of use, but only so far as necessary, and he has determined that the use should be common.'[2] Later, Ambrose of Milan (*c.* 340–397 CE) wrote that in charity 'you are giving the poor man what is his' for the goods of the earth are given for the 'common use of everyone'.[3]

We explore the preferential place of the poor more closely in Chapter 7. For now, we have seen the scriptural basis for a common destination for goods, based on the doctrine of creation. As God created all things, so he created them for everyone. This notion is brought out more strongly in the witness of Clement and Ambrose, but it also finds roots in Scripture.

Throughout Scripture we find the poor have a special place in God's favour and concern. Here we can note that the sharing of goods in common gives us one example of a manner of living which finds divine favour. In Isaiah we find the injunction to share food with those who are hungry, shelter the homeless, clothe the naked, because they are fellow members of the human family.[4]

We have seen already how Matthew 25 demands such actions because of humanity's participation in Christ. The Common Good is the practical outworking of this dignity.

Common Good/s

The Common Good is appealed to in Catholic Social Teaching in various senses. We shall now uncover these various senses before turning to consider the relationship between the Common Good and ownership of goods or property. At times, the Common Good is appealed to in such a way that the nature of the 'good' involved is not always obvious – whether it is speaking about abstract morality, or concrete 'goods'.

Leo XIII, in *Rerum Novarum*, is the first to use the term 'Common Good'. It has thus been a feature of Catholic Social Teaching from the outset. Here the Common Good is defined as 'the interests of all in general, albeit with individual interests also in their due place and degree'.[5] It is not defined more precisely at this stage. There is a recognition that the Common Good exists alongside individual interests, and also that the contribution of individuals to the Common Good will be dependent upon ability: 'It should not be supposed that all can contribute in the like way and to the same extent.'[6] There is no clear means given of deciding when an individual interest must be maintained or when the Common Good demands an individual contribute more according to their ability.

Pius XI, writing in *Quadragesimo Anno*, goes further. Freedom of action is maintained 'on condition that the Common Good be preserved and wrong to any individual abolished'.[7] The Common Good is preserved when actions are performed which do not do wrong to other individuals. Or, in other terms, if an action wrongs another individual it does not contribute towards the Common Good. He also defines the Common Good as 'social justice', understood as overcoming the disparities that exist between those who have an excess of goods and those who have nothing at all. The Common Good is not served where surplus is built up by one individual or community, while another individual or community remains in serious want.

The Common Good is therefore 'intimately bound up with human nature', according to John XXIII.[8] He notes that it exists only when the dignity of the human person is taken into account at all times. The Common Good is not served where people are instrumentalized and not treated in accordance with the dignity we described in the previous chapter.

The Fathers of the Second Vatican Council define the Common Good in terms of human fulfilment as 'the sum of those conditions of social life which allow social groups and their individual members relatively thorough and ready access to their own fulfillment'.[9] John Paul II also affirms the relation of the Common Good to dignity, but insists that the Common Good 'is not simply the sum total of particular interests; rather it involves an assessment and integration of those interests'.[10] The Common Good ensures that the good of each person is preserved, and adjudicated upon with the principle of human dignity as the deciding factor.

The Common Good is a shared pursuit and the duty of the entire human family. It is therefore strongly linked to the principle of solidarity we will consider in the next chapter. The Common Good belongs 'to everyone and to each person, it is and remains "common", because it is indivisible and because only together is it possible to attain it, increase it and safeguard its effectiveness'.[11]

Private Property and Common Good

We have seen that within Scripture there are passages which seem to suggest that property should be held in common. At the very least, we have seen that there is a basis in Scripture for the common use of property, when an individual is in need.

An example will help us here. I have two loaves of bread which I produced or purchased. If I fill my belly with one loaf while the family next to me have none, I am not fulfilling the obligation placed on me by this tradition within Scripture. If we follow the logic of Acts 4, I should not have claimed private ownership of the loaves at all. Acts 2 might suggest I should sell the extra loaf to give the money to the family next door, while Isaiah tells me that I should give the extra loaf to my neighbour in need.

Can I say that the loaf in question is mine? Within the Catholic tradition before *Rerum Novarum*, the question is disputed. While private property was often assumed, St Thomas questions the right to own private property without qualification.

Eduardo Peñalver describes Thomas' antipathy toward property: 'He never treats it as a natural right, but instead remains largely within the patristic tradition that treats private ownership as, at most, permissible for prudential reasons.'[12]

However, Peñalver also notes that Thomas presents a subtle shift from the patristic tradition, as the prudential reasons given by Thomas offer 'a more affirmative account' of property ownership. Private property is defended by Thomas in *Summa Theologica* as the best means of administration of Common Goods for three reasons. First, it encourages procurement of goods, as 'every man is more careful to procure what is for himself alone'; second, because common ownership can cause confusion; and third, because it is more peaceful when some amount of personal property is condoned: 'It is to be observed that quarrels arise more frequently where there is no division of the things possessed.'[13]

While private property is defended as the best means of administration of goods, it is not absolute. Aquinas goes on to conclude: 'On this respect man ought to possess external things, not as his own, but as common, so that, to wit, he is ready to communicate them to others in their need.'[14] Ownership of property is private, in the sense that it is not communal. However, it is not private in the sense that another in need has a right to that property. It might therefore better be described as 'personal' property, than private property outright. Persons have the right to possessions, but they are not private to them. Rather, persons act as stewards or custodians of whatever good, until such a time as another with a need for that good presents themselves. In this case, the 'owner' must be ready to communicate the good to the person in need.[15]

The first document of Catholic Social Teaching presents a substantial change in the understanding of private property. Leo

XIII for the first time declares private ownership 'the natural right of man'.[16] In terms of authority, he cites Thomas Aquinas. However, the citation Leo uses is the one we have already discussed. Leo glosses the text to argue that such ownership is 'not only lawful, but absolutely necessary'.[17] However, he goes on to say that there is a corresponding duty alongside this right, also quoting Aquinas, to suggest that goods should be used as if 'common to all'. Leo affirms the right to private property, but also the obligation to use that property for the Common Good.

In fact, Leo is insistent that the argument from creation that might suggest common ownership of property should not be applied: 'The fact that God has given the earth for the use and enjoyment of the whole human race can in no way be a bar to the owning of private property.'[18] Private ownership is for the first time regarded as a 'law of nature'.[19]

What explains this insistence, which seems at odds with a tradition which is hesitant to affirm private ownership outright? Here the context of the letter becomes important. The letter is written at a time when 'the spirit of revolutionary change' was sweeping across Europe and the West.[20] *Rerum Novarum* is written both to discourage the faithful from seeking revolutionary solutions to the problems besetting the newly industrialized nations, and to provide solutions to those problems in order to render the appeal of other solutions less attractive.

Socialism is a constant target throughout the letter, and a defence of private property becomes a means to undermine the appeal of socialism by refuting one of its tenets. Some socialists had taken against all private property, echoing the words of Pierre-Joseph Proudhon: 'Property is robbery!'[21] Leo writes: 'To remedy these wrongs the socialists, working on the poor man's envy of the rich, are striving to do away with private property, and contend that individual possessions should become the common property of all.'[22]

In order to counter the appeal of socialism, Leo renders private property not just a permissible means of good order, but a natural right. As such, it is not admissible 'to lay violent hands on other people's possessions'.[23] To do so would now constitute an assault of a 'right' to property. For Aquinas, failure to render property to common use when confronted with need 'inflicts the same kind of injury as taking a thing unjustly'.[24] With Leo XIII's declaration of private property as a right, it is less clear that failure to use that property for the benefit of all is an equivalent action to taking it unjustly.

As the threat of forms of socialism seeking to abolish all property subsided over the course of the twentieth century, various Popes re-emphasized the duty to use property for the Common Good, while maintaining such property as a 'right'. They defend this 'right' on the advantages property confers in the functioning of society, those same reasons to which St Thomas had pointed while demonstrating why such ownership was permissible.

We see this from as early as *Quadragesimo Anno*. Pius XI rebalances the status of private property as a 'right' alongside the 'duty' of use for the Common Good. He describes the 'twofold character of ownership, called usually individual or social according as it regards either separate persons or the Common Good'.[25] God has both 'given man the right of private ownership not only that individuals may be able to provide for themselves . . . but also that the goods which the Creator destined for the entire family of mankind may through this institution truly serve this purpose'.[26] Like Leo, Pius overemphasizes the extent to which previous theologians have been unanimous in affirming property as a right.

However, Pius goes further than Leo in reaffirming the duty towards the Common Good. Pius notes that public authorities 'can determine more accurately upon consideration of the true requirements of the Common Good, what is permitted and what is not permitted to owners in the use of their property'.[27] Leo's earlier fears about the nature of such intervention give way to an enhanced role of the State to help individuals make use of the private property for the Common Good. In doing so, it 'prevents the private possession of goods . . . from causing intolerable evils and thus rushing to its own destruction . . . but safeguards them; and it does not weaken private property rights, but strengthens them'.[28]

The Second Vatican Council went further still, allowing public authorities to transfer goods into public ownership for the Common Good, providing fair compensation is offered.[29] They also give the State a role in policing the use of private goods, allowing the State the right 'to prevent anyone from abusing his private property to the detriment of the Common Good'.[30] Suppose, for example, a wealthy individual is buying properties in an area but not letting them, especially in order to drive up or maintain prices in that area by limiting available housing stock, this right might permit a public authority to intervene for the Common Good of those who need to live and work affordably in that area.

Finally, John Paul II makes clear this trajectory away from a more or less absolute right to private property: 'The right to private property is subordinated to the right to common use, to the fact that goods are meant for everyone.'[31] The *Compendium* cements this position: 'Christian tradition has never recognized the right to private property as absolute and untouchable.'[32] Instead, we find the nature of private goods described as having a 'universal destination'.[33] The universal destination of goods is an invitation to remind people that nothing was created for private use or enjoyment, but always to be used 'so as to bring about a world of fairness and solidarity'.

Catholic Social Teaching thus charts a course between private property as an absolute right and common ownership as an absolute duty. Personal property is encouraged but with various caveats. It is not encouraged without restriction, but so that 'all classes of people' may have access to 'secure, even if modest, property'.[34] Personal ownership is favoured as the best means of administration of private property, but that ownership is limited to the direction of the Common Good. The Common Good is the universal destination of all goods.

Common Good and the Role of the State

The Common Good is frequently related to the role of the State within Catholic Social Teaching. From as early as *Rerum*

Novarum, the role of those in power is linked to serving 'the Common Good', with particular reference to the interests of the poor.[35] John XXIII identified the realization of the Common Good as the State's 'whole raison d'être'.[36] Elsewhere, he describes 'the attainment of the Common Good [as] the sole reason for the existence of civil authorities'.[37]

Catholic Social Teaching recognizes a conflicted role for the State in relation to the Common Good and private property. On the one hand, it notes that the Common Good can demand State and public ownership to ensure that the goods of the earth are shared more commonly with all. We have already seen the role Pius XI allows the State in deciding how privately owned property might better serve the Common Good.[38] In *Mater et Magistra*, this role is confirmed, 'explained by the exigencies of the Common Good, which demand that the public authority broaden its sphere of activity'.[39]

On the other hand, however, the principle of subsidiarity (which we explore in detail below) is also invoked to curb the influence of the State appropriately, so that it does not harm the Common Good and reduce private property entirely or 'beyond measure'.[40]

The Common Good is the yardstick by which it will be decided whether the State's intervention in the distribution of private property is considered just. The disparity between the few exceedingly rich and the many without property 'must be effectively called back to and brought into conformity with the norms of the Common Good, that is, social justice'.[41] This role for the State is not redistribution of wealth to the point of equality, nor even necessarily to an entirely fair distribution of resources, but to safeguard a modest amount of property for those without property so that they too might share in a moderate amount of wealth. The tradition is silent on what is the best mechanism for achieving such a redistribution. However, as we shall see below, subsidiarity as a principle is key in understanding who is to decide on such distribution.

We have already seen how the living wage is a feature within Catholic Social Thought as a right arising out of the human dignity of the worker. The right to a living wage is also seen as a means to safeguard the Common Good, as 'it helps the Common Good for workers and other employees, by setting aside some part of their income which remains after necessary expenditures, to attain gradually to the possession of moderate wealth'.[42] Rates of pay should be such that they afford the worker comfort as befits their dignity, with surplus to enable the worker to save a small amount. In many developed economies we are observing a rise in the cost of living, while wages stagnate or even fall in real terms. John Paul II points out that wages are also related to the Common Good as for most people they are the means by which they have any access to the goods destined for common use.[43]

John XXIII recognizes that wages must be set carefully, 'having regard especially to the repercussions on the overall employment of the working force in the country as a whole . . . within the limits of the Common Good'.[44] Setting wages too high, too quickly, can lead to unemployment if the company as a whole cannot afford such a wage bill. However, as a general rule 'wages too shall increase'.[45]

The last 30 years have seen a large increase in wage ratios between those paid the most and those paid the least. For example, in the United States in 2016 CEOs in America's largest firms made on average $15.6 million. The Economic Policy Institute notes that this is '271 times the annual average pay of the typical worker . . . light years beyond the 20-to-1 ratio in 1965 and the 59-to-1 ratio in 1989'.[46] Catholic Social Teaching demands that when there is money to increase wages at the highest level 'wages too shall increase' for every worker in line with the Common Good.

This increase in executive pay and the standard of living for the exceedingly rich has contributed to the findings of the first ever World Inequality Report which found that 'in recent decades, income inequality has increased in nearly all countries'.[47] The rate of increase has been particularly dramatic in the United States of America where the top 1 per cent of income share made up 20 per cent of total income, revealing staggering levels of income disparity.[48] Some economists suggest the price of such increased levels of inequality is high, as it can lead to political and social instability, and a decline in quality of life through rising crime and decreased access to educational and other opportunities for social wellbeing.[49]

Catholic Social Teaching, since *Quadragesimo Anno*, has warned against capital hiring labour in a manner which benefits itself in the short term, but violates the good of every person within the economic system: 'It does violate right order when capital hires workers, that is, the non-owning working class, with a view to and under such terms that it directs business and even the whole economic system according to its own will and advantage, scorning the human dignity of the workers, the social character of economic activity and social justice itself, and the Common Good.'[50]

John XXIII writes with words which should have acted as a prophetic clarion against ever-increasing returns for the wealthiest: 'Demands of the Common Good, both on a national and a world level, must also be borne in mind when assessing the rate of return due as compensation to the company's management.'[51] He insisted on 'care lest privileged classes arise, even among the workers'.[52]

Instead, Catholic Social Thought suggests a role for the State and, given the increasingly global nature of corporations, other transnational bodies to mediate between the interests of every person in the economic system. The justification for this role and 'of all government action is the Common Good . . . Everything must be done to ensure that citizens of the less developed areas are treated as responsible human beings, and are allowed to play the major role in achieving their own economic, social and cultural advancement.'[53]

The findings of the World Inequality Report suggest that such intervention might bear fruit, as inequality is rising in different countries 'at different speeds, suggesting that institutions and policies matter in shaping inequality'.[54] According to the principle of the Common Good, then, Catholic Social Teaching suggests that the State should 'adjust their legislation to meet the requirements of the given situation'.[55] This means finding appropriate legislation not only at national but also international level. As John XXIII noted: 'In the past rulers of States seem to have been able to make sufficient provision for the universal Common Good through the normal diplomatic channels . . . by using, that is, the ways and means suggested by the natural law, the law of nations, or international law.'[56] This is not only negative, condemning or prohibiting bad practice, but positive, encouraging and helping to promote best practice, as Pope Francis notes, 'to stimulate creativity in seeking new solutions and to encourage individual or group initiatives'.[57]

John XXIII was writing in 1963. He noted that even then 'the universal Common Good presents us with problems which are world-wide in their dimensions; problems, therefore, which cannot be solved except by a public authority with power, organization and means co-extensive with these problems, and with a world-wide sphere of activity'.[58]

Gaudium et Spes notes likewise, shortly after John XXIII, that the Common Good has taken on an 'increasingly universal complexion and consequently involves rights and duties with respect to the whole human race'.[59] Since then, the growth in inter- and trans-national corporations has only increased the need for a collective effort on the part of nation states to work together for the universal Common Good. Recently, Pope Francis recognizes 'that some economic sectors exercise more power than states themselves'.[60] Pope Francis describes these powers elsewhere 'who reject the right of states, charged with vigilance for the Common Good, to exercise any form of control. A new tyranny is thus born, invisible and often virtual, which unilaterally and relentlessly imposes its own laws and rules.'[61]

To overcome this tyranny, Catholic Social Teaching has long suggested international collaboration to safeguard the Common Good and to overcome the inability of individual States in the face of this 'new tyranny'. John Paul II held that 'it is necessary that there be increased coordination among the more powerful countries, and that in international agencies the interests of the whole human family be equally represented'.[62]

As we shall see below when we explore subsidiarity, the current rise in self-interested nationalism therefore poses a potential risk to the universal Common Good. Pope John Paul II condemned such nationalism as detrimental to the Common Good: 'If a nation were to succumb more or less deliberately to the temptation to close in upon itself and failed to meet the responsibilities following from its superior position in the community of nations, it would fall seriously short of its clear ethical duty.'[63]

However, the Common Good is not a matter for the nation state alone. It is the reason for its existence, but it is not the only actor in society which has the Common Good as its concern. Pope Francis notes that 'society as a whole, and the state in particular, are obliged to defend and promote the Common Good'.[64]

While it is the State's duty in particular, it is a duty for each and every one of us in society to act in such a way as to promote the Common Good. According to the *Compendium*, 'no one is exempt from cooperating, according to each one's possibilities, in attaining' the Common Good.[65]

Common Good and the Individual

The Common Good demands we face some hard truths. Almost all of us are living examples of the kind of individualism prophesied by Paul VI 'in which each one claims his own rights without wishing to be answerable for the Common Good'.[66]

If those of us who have more, and are better off, are genuinely concerned about the Common Good, it will mean that we are called to give up some, if not most, of our wealth in the service of those who have less. *Mater et Magistra* describes how the Common Good may sometimes require 'subordination of individual and group interests to the interest of the Common Good as the principal remedies for these evils'.[67]

If you're wondering whether that's you, almost everyone who reads this book will be considerably better off than many in the human family. It will require discipline and will to genuinely serve the Common Good with all the many things we have and own. It will require discipline and will to fly in the face of the spirit of an age that tells us our ultimate meaning is found in the stuff we can accumulate for ourselves.

Almost all of those reading these pages, including the one writing these words, enjoys the myth of an affluent lifestyle, at the expense of those both poorer in our home nation and especially in those countries which are less economically 'developed'. Pope Francis delivered this message to an audience of young people: 'The poverty of the world is a scandal. In a world where there is such great wealth, so many resources for giving food to everyone, it is impossible to understand how there could be so many hungry children, so many children without education, so many poor people! . . . We must all think about whether we can become a little poorer.'[68]

Later in the same audience, Pope Francis describes the demands of the Common Good on the individual: 'Involvement in politics is an obligation for a Christian. We Christians cannot "play the role of Pilate", washing our hands of it; we cannot. We must be involved in politics because politics is one of the highest forms of charity for it seeks the Common Good.'[69]

The message of Catholic Social Teaching is clear. While politicians might not do God, God demands Christians do politics. The commitment to the Common Good demanded by Catholic Social Teaching sometimes requires entry into the political arena. It does so because the raison d'être of the State and of politics is the Common Good of the whole *polis*, the Common Good of the whole human family. Christians cannot therefore avoid this essential means of furthering the Common Good.

Public participation in the Common Good is not limited to politics. Pope Francis has also suggested smaller ways that all of us can be involved in the Common Good of our locality. This could be something as simple as showing 'concern for a public place (a building, a fountain, an abandoned monument, a landscape, a square), and strive to protect, restore, improve or beautify it as something belonging to everyone'.[70]

This can, in turn, develop into a more thoroughgoing involvement in the Common Good, as individuals develop their capacity to act. Small success at the local level can develop participation in efforts to serve the Common Good on a larger scale. For example, many of those involved in the Living Wage campaign in Britain, which has seen many businesses pay a voluntary minimum wage which accurately reflects the cost of living, began with some small-scale victories. These small victories increased participation and the ability of the campaign to bring a just wage to many others.[71]

Common Good and the Future

Which human beings are counted in the Common Good? It is obvious from what we have said so far that each and every human currently alive is included within the Common Good. Decisions can't be made for the benefit of one section or group within the human family that wrong another. This means, for example, that one nation state can't enjoy economic success and a good standard of living at the expense of another. John XXIII reminded us that 'the demands of the Common Good on the international level include: the avoidance of all forms of unfair competition between the economies of different countries . . . and effective co-operation in the development of economically less advanced communities.'[72]

However, a repeated feature of the principle within Catholic Social Teaching is to widen the scope of the Common Good to include those not yet born. *Mater et Magistra* states that progress in living standards can only be made in such a way 'seeing to it that the benefits which make possible a more human way of life will be available not merely to the present generation but to the coming generations as well'.[73] Pope Francis has repeated this extended focus: 'The Common Good also extends to future generations . . . since the world we have received also belongs to those who will follow us.'[74]

Even among the human family alive today, we see short-term interests of one group or section of people being prioritized at the expense of others. When the demands of the Common Good of future generations are taken into account we are especially aware of failings.

Instead of taking the interests of the whole of humanity, present and future, into account, Pope Francis notes how politicians are rather 'concerned with immediate results, supported by consumerist sectors of the population . . . driven to produce short-term growth. In response to electoral interests, governments are reluctant to upset the public with measures which could affect the level of consumption.'[75] He calls instead for 'true statecraft' which thinks of the 'long-term Common Good' and notes that opportunities for this statecraft have, even in recent times, been missed: 'The financial crisis of 2007–08 provided an opportunity to develop a new economy, more attentive to ethical principles, and new ways of regulating speculative financial practices and virtual wealth. But the response to the crisis did not include rethinking the outdated criteria which continue to rule the world.'[76]

Nowhere is the relationship between the current human family and future generations clearer with respect to the Common Good than in terms of the environment. This is the overarching theme of Pope Francis' *Laudato Si'*. He points out that the environment is a good example of a Common Good 'belonging to all and meant for all'.[77] Instead of the Common Good being the focus of environmental policy, 'There are too many special interests, and economic interests easily end up trumping the common good and manipulating information so that their own plans will not be affected'.[78]

Short- to medium-term gains in relation to convenience and supply are being prioritized over the long-term Common Good, which requires we carefully steward limited resources and environment. The Common Good demands that we prioritize the long-term dignity of every human, even those yet to be born, over the short-term interests of a privileged few of those living now.

Common Good in the Church

What of the Common Good in the Church? We shall explore what a Church which adheres to the Common Good might look like in our final chapter. For now, we can focus on the relationship between the Church and the Common Good in two respects. First, the Church's role in promoting the Common Good, and, second, the role of the Common Good between communities and organizations which make up the Church.

We have seen throughout the above chapter that the human family is sorely in need of being reminded of the nature of the Common Good. Whether it's our increasingly isolated or individualistic ways of living, our accumulation of more stuff than we could ever possibly use or need, we are all prioritizing ourselves over the Common Good. Almost all of us reading these words are enjoying a quality of life based on the diminishing of others, through outsourcing or through the consequences our actions will have on the planet and future generations.

Pope Francis notes that 'development is impossible without upright men and women, without financiers and politicians whose consciences are finely attuned to the requirements of the Common Good'.[79] One role the Church has to play with respect to the Common Good is to be a place where we are training those men and women, financiers and politicians, whose duty it is to safeguard the Common Good. As Christians, our churches should be cradles of communality, where the skills and practices of the Common Good are nurtured and caught, and so passed between generations.

This extends to the relationship within Christian communities and churches. As Churches and Christian communities we too should be committed to the Common Good, which means putting the money and resources that have been entrusted to us to the service of those who need them.

Philip North gives us an example of Christian communities failing to live in accordance with the Common Good even among themselves. He draws attention to the disparity between dioceses within one Christian denomination in the United Kingdom.[80] Across the dioceses which make up the Church of England, the richest diocese holds funds of £209.40 per head and the poorest £25 per head, based in part on historical assets of the particular dioceses. North suggests that these assets should be redistributed to better serve the Common Good, by allowing them to be deployed according to need instead of historic accident. This is but one example of a Christian community which is not modelling a radical commitment to the Common Good among its brothers and sisters in Christ, let alone the whole human family.

The Church and all Christian communities are called upon to model a commitment to the Common Good for the sake of the Common Good of the entire human family. This can be difficult. It's costly, and means giving up sole access to useful resources which we have accumulated in the course of life and ministry, and entrusting them to other brothers and sisters in Christ, and beyond. One of the difficulties in this pursuit of the Common Good is that we become enablers of people of good will who might look and think very differently from us. One of the reasons for their different thoughts and looks is that disparity in wealth can create very different appearances and points of view. Pursuing the Common Good opens us to be challenged by them, and to recognize in them, even if we disagree, the presence of Christ anew.

No doubt it was difficult for the early Christians, who made up the communities referred to at the beginning of Acts, to relinquish their assets and put them to the wider use of the community according to need. Jesus told the rich young man he lacked one thing, and to sell what he owned to give the money to the poor (Mark 10.21–23). When the rich young man heard this he was shocked and went away grieving. To be committed to the Common Good is not an easy task, especially when we have become so bloated and find our identity in our many possessions and financial successes. If the Church is to lead the way in reorienting the whole human race towards the

Common Good (and in particular if 'successful' branches of the Church whose success is based in part on access to finance and resources are to lead the way in this) as Christians, we too lack one thing.

Notes

1 *Populorum*, 23, citing S. Ambrose, *On Naboth*, 12.53. McGuire, M. R. P., 'De Nabuthae', *Patristic Studies* 15 (1927), 46–103.

2 Clement of Alexandria, *Paedagogus* 38 (2.13), available at: http://www.newadvent.org/fathers/02092.htm (accessed 1 May 2018).

3 *On Naboth*, 12.53.

4 Isaiah 58.6–8; see further King, N. and Rowe, J., *Calling People of Goodwill: The Bible and the Common Good* (Bible Society, 2017).

5 *Rerum*, 51.

6 *Rerum*, 34.

7 *Quadragesimo*, 25.

8 *Pacem*, 55.

9 *Gaudium*, 26; see also *Gaudium*, 74.

10 *Centesimus*, 47.

11 *Compendium*, 164.

12 Peñalver, E., 'Catholic & Libertarian?' in *Commonweal* 141.12 (2014), 13–15.

13 St Thomas Aquinas, *Summa Theologica* 2.2.66, available at: http://www.newadvent.org/summa/3066.htm (accessed 25 August 2018).

14 *Summa Theologica* 2.2.66.

15 See further White, R. S., 'Appendix: Aquinas on the right to own private property' in *Natural Law in English Renaissance Literature* (Cambridge: Cambridge University Press, 1996), 252–5.

16 *Rerum*, 22.

17 *Rerum*, 22.

18 *Rerum*, 8.

19 *Rerum*, 9.

20 *Rerum*, 1.

21 Proudhon, J. P., *What is Property? An Inquiry into the Principle of Right and Government* (1840).

22 *Rerum*, 4.

23 *Rerum*, 38.

24 *Summa Theologica* 2.2.66.

25 *Quadragesimo*, 45.

26 *Quadragesimo*, 45.

27 *Quadragesimo*, 49.

28 *Quadragesimo*, 49.

29 *Gaudium*, 71.
30 *Gaudium*, 71.
31 *Laborem*, 14.
32 *Compendium*, 177.
33 *Compendium*, 174.
34 Pius XII, cited in *Mater*, 114.
35 *Rerum*, 32.
36 *Mater*, 20.
37 *Pacem*, 54.
38 *Quadragesimo*, 49.
39 *Mater*, 117.
40 *Mater*, 117.
41 *Quadragesimo*, 58.
42 *Quadragesimo*, 74.
43 *Laborem*, 19.
44 *Mater*, 71.
45 *Mater*, 71; see also *Gaudium*, 67; *Laborem*, 19.
46 Mishel, L., Schieder, J., 'CEO pay remains high relative to the pay of typical workers and high-wage earners' (Washington, DC: Economic Policy Institute 2017), available at: https://www.epi.org/files/pdf/130354.pdf (accessed 4 January 2018).
47 Alvarado, F., Chancel, L., Piketty, T., Saez, E., Zucman, G., *World Inequality Report 2018*, 9, available at: https://wir2018.wid.world/files/download/wir2018-full-report-english.pdf (accessed 20 August 2018). Pope Francis reflects on this trend in *Evangelii Gaudium* (56): 'While the earnings of a minority are growing exponentially, so too is the gap separating the majority from the prosperity enjoyed by those happy few. This imbalance is the result of ideologies which defend the absolute autonomy of the marketplace and financial speculation.'
48 *World Inequality Report*, 10.
49 See further, Stiglitz, J., *The Price of Inequality* (London: Penguin, 2013) and Piketty, T., *Capital in the Twenty-First Century* (Harvard, MA: Harvard University Press, 2014) and *The Economics of Inequality* (Harvard, MA: Harvard University Press, 2015).
50 *Quadragesimo*, 101.
51 *Mater*, 81.
52 *Mater*, 79.
53 *Mater*, 151.
54 *World Inequality Report*, 9.
55 *Pacem*, 54.
56 *Pacem*, 133.
57 *Laudato*, 177.
58 *Pacem*, 137.
59 *Gaudium*, 26.
60 *Laudato*, 196.

61 *Evangelii Gaudium*, 56.

62 *Centesimus*, 58.

63 *Sollicitudo*, 23.

64 *Laudato*, 157.

65 *Compendium*, 167.

66 *Octogesima*, 23.

67 *Mater*, 37.

68 Pope Francis, 'Address of Pope Francis to the Students of Jesuit Schools in Italy and Albania' (7 June 2013), available at: http://w2.vatican.va/content/francesco/en/speeches/2013/june/documents/papa-francesco_20130607_scuole-gesuiti.html (accessed 21 August 2018). Likewise John Paul II suggested: 'This may mean making important changes in established life-styles, in order to limit the waste of environmental and human resources' (*Centesimus*, 52).

69 Pope Francis, 'Address of Pope Francis to the Students of Jesuit Schools'.

70 *Laudato*, 232.

71 For the history of the Living Wage Campaign in Britain, see Bolton, M., *How to Resist* (London: Bloomsbury, 2018) and Heery, E., Hann, D., Nash, D., 'The Living Wage Campaign in the UK' in *Employee Relations* 39.6 (2017), 800–14.

72 *Mater*, 80.

73 *Mater*, 79.

74 *Laudato*, 159.

75 *Laudato*, 178.

76 *Laudato*, 189.

77 *Laudato*, 23.

78 *Laudato*, 54.

79 *Evangelii Gaudium*, 71.

80 North, P., 'The spreadsheet or the cross – time to choose' in *The Church Times* (1 June 2018), available at: https://www.churchtimes.co.uk/articles/2018/1-june/comment/opinion/the-spreadsheet-or-the-cross-time-to-choose (accessed 20 August 2018).

4

Solidarity

> The word 'solidarity' is a little worn and at times poorly understood, but it refers to something more than a few sporadic acts of generosity. It presumes the creation of a new mindset which thinks in terms of community and the priority of the life of all over the appropriation of goods by a few.[1]

Unlike subsidiarity, the focus of our next chapter, solidarity is a familiar word. It is so familiar that we sometimes take that we understand what solidarity demands for granted. As Pope Francis puts it, the word is 'a little worn'.

The principle of solidarity is found clearly on the pages of Scripture. It is underlined by the relation we have to one another in Christ. We're so used to hearing that we have a relation together in the body of Christ that we sometimes fail to think through what this relationship might mean.

If solidarity is the principle which is most familiar to us, it is also the principle which we violate most easily, especially in the modern world. Very few of us truly act as if we were members one of another. Mostly, we exist in our silos and tribes. We act according to the prevailing individualism of the world in which we live. We act as if there's no such thing as society. We put ourselves first.

We will explore how the principle of solidarity challenges such individualism. First we look at the scriptural basis of the principle, before turning to the principle as it is found within Catholic Social Teaching.

Scriptural Basis

The scriptural basis for the principle of solidarity is Christological. It stems from the solidarity all baptized Christians have as members of Christ's body, and from the solidarity we enjoy as human beings, brought into relationship with each other, because of Christ's becoming a human being.

He did not count 'equality with God as something to be exploited, but emptied himself, taking the form of a slave, being born in human likeness' (Phil. 2.6–7). In the incarnation God sided with us, entering into our state. The solidarity that God expresses with us binds us together. He enters into solidarity with us, and through that solidarity, we enter into solidarity with each other.

Throughout St Paul's letters, and the letters attributed to him, the 'body of Christ' is an important theological concept. The 'body of Christ' as expressed in these letters is the foundation of the principle of solidarity. Paul's description of the 'body of Christ' occurs in several places.[2] In Romans 12.5, he describes how 'we, who are many, are one body in Christ, and individually we are members one of another'. The author of the letter to the Ephesians reminds us that this means that we are members of others who might be very different to us. Race does not divide us, but we are members of the same body even across racial and ethnic 'divides': 'Gentiles have become fellow-heirs, members of the same body' (Eph 3.6).

In his first letter to the Corinthians he draws out the consequences of our being members of the body and one another. He writes, 'if one member suffers, all suffer together with it; if one member is honoured, all rejoice together with it' (1 Cor. 12.26). This is the best articulation of the principle of solidarity in Scripture.

St Paul reminds us that we are bound together, and the relation between us constitutes the solidarity found in Catholic Social Teaching. The consequences of this are profound. If there is another human being in suffering, we are suffering too. If there is another human being in misery, solidarity demands that we do whatever it is in our power to alleviate it. Our solidarity means that we should not rest content while others suffer.

These two scriptural bases, our solidarity because of God's solidarity with us, and solidarity among Christians as fellow members of the body, come together in the Eucharist. The Fathers of the Second Vatican Council draw this connection in *Gaudium et Spes*: 'The Lord left behind a pledge of this hope and strength for life's journey in that sacrament of faith where natural elements refined by man are gloriously changed into His Body and Blood, providing a meal of brotherly solidarity and a foretaste of the heavenly banquet.'[3]

In his first letter to the Corinthians, St Paul asks: 'The cup of blessing that we bless, is it not a sharing in the blood of Christ? The bread that we break, is it not a sharing in the body of Christ?' (1 Cor. 10.16).

Christ has pledged his solidarity with us: 'Where two or three are gathered in my name, I am there among them' (Matt. 18.20). Nowhere is this more true than in the Eucharist. Each and every time we celebrate the Eucharist, Christ once again enters into solidarity with humanity through the gift of himself, 'this is my body . . . this is my blood' (Mark 14.22, 24). As we participate in the Eucharist, Christ strengthens the solidarity between us as fellow members of his body. Companions share communion. Sharing bread with each other, the literal meaning of *com-panion*, becomes the means by which we are united together into *comm-union*. We strengthen the ties of solidarity that link us as one human family in the one body of Christ.

Solidarity in Catholic Social Teaching

It might appear odd that 'solidarity' emerged as a principle of Catholic Social Teaching at all. Pope Benedict (when Joseph Ratzinger) noted that the word comes from outside the Christian tradition.[4] Originally a legal term referring to joint culpability with respect to a debt or obligation, the term obtains its modern sense in the writing of the early socialist Pierre Leroux.[5] Indeed, as Ratzinger notes, Leroux uses the concept in direct 'contraposition to the Christian idea of love as the new, rational and effective response to social problems'.[6] Leroux contrasts the 'solidarity' of true love with the 'duty' of Christian love. Lawrence Wilde notes for Leroux solidarity entailed people 'embracing their fellow human beings in mutually supportive relations'.[7]

'Solidarity' is found in several documents of Catholic Social Teaching. It is first used, as we shall see, by John XXIII in *Mater et Magistra*. However, it becomes established as a principle of Catholic Social Teaching through John Paul II's use of the term in *Sollicitudo Rei Socialis*.

John Paul's use of the term is perhaps not surprising given his Polish origin and his association with the Polish trade union, Solidarność (Solidarity) led by Lech Walesa. Justin Welby notes that the word solidarity 'sprang into popular consciousness' through its association with this trade union.[8]

This Polish association explains John Paul II's fondness for the term, despite its initial anti-Christian usage by Leroux. John Paul II pointed to Solidarność as a model of the struggle for political freedom and human rights. We see his fondness for the movement in a homily given at the place where it was founded: 'In the name of mankind and of humanity, the word "solidarity" must be pronounced . . . This word was uttered right here, in a new way and in a new context.'[9] He notes the significance of this proclamation: 'How significant is the fact, that this very word – "solidarity" – was voiced right here.'[10]

The importance of the concept for John Paul II is clear. Writing in *Centesimus Annus*, he describes the principle of solidarity as 'one of the fundamental principles of the Christian view of social and political organization'.[11] Although he finds thematic precursors from the earliest days of Catholic Social Teaching in Leo XIII's use of 'friendly concord' between rich and poor in *Rerum Novarum*, and Pius XI's use of the term 'social charity' in *Quadragesimo Anno*, John Paul II is ultimately responsible for the term's continued use in Catholic Social Teaching.[12]

The term 'solidarity' does feature in the earlier Catholic Social Teaching that emerges around the time of the Second Vatican Council. It emerges in the context of industrial relations and disparity between rich and poor nations. John XXIII calls on workers and employers to organize 'their mutual relations in accordance with the principle of human solidarity and Christian brotherhood'.[13] The same solidarity which should improve relations in the workplace places an obligation on wealthy nations to do more to support those countries which lack similar resources: 'The solidarity which binds all men together as members of a common family makes it impossible for wealthy nations to look with indifference upon the hunger, misery and poverty of other nations whose citizens are unable to enjoy even elementary human rights.'[14] In *Pacem in Terris* he repeats this call for wealthy nations to cultivate an 'active solidarity' by 'taking positive steps to pool their material and spiritual resources'.[15]

The Fathers of the Second Vatican Council stress that 'solidarity with the whole social organism' does not inhibit 'personal initiative'.[16] Acting in solidarity with our fellow human beings does not mean we cannot take personal initiative or act creatively, only that we must not do so at their expense or in violation of the Common Good.

Paul VI writes further on the obligations that solidarity brings: 'We are under obligation to all men . . . the reality of human solidarity brings us not only benefits but also obligations.'[17] We have already seen above the obligation which the Common Good places on us to consider those who come after us.

Paul VI also makes use of the concept of solidarity in relations between nations, in a manner similar to John XXIII. He describes the obligation of 'mutual solidarity' wealthier nations are under with respect to poorer nations.[18] He condemns nationalism and racism as 'obstacles to creation of a more just social order and to the development of world solidarity'.[19]

We shall discuss nationalism in more detail in the following chapter. For now, we note that solidarity implies an obligation in respect of nations in need or poorer than our own. We are living through a moment in history in which nations are increasingly seeking to reap the benefits of international relations, while reneging on the obligations those benefits place on us. National governments enjoy the economic benefits that migration brings but demonize the migrants who provide that boost. Nations fail to fulfil international obligations regarding the acceptance of refugees, while treating those fleeing conflict with suspicion. All of these represent failures of solidarity.

Paul VI reminds us of our duty to welcome refugees and economic migrants: 'We cannot insist too much on the duty of giving foreigners a hospitable reception. It is a duty imposed by human solidarity and by Christian charity, and it is incumbent upon families and educational institutions in the host nations.'[20] He notes that this solidarity cannot be taken for granted, but must be supported through 'a renewed education'.[21] Failure to train individuals in the obligations of solidarity 'can give rise to an individualism in which each one claims his own rights without wishing to be answerable for the Common Good'.[22]

We now move to consider the principle of solidarity as articulated by John Paul II, who, as we have said, is the most responsible for the principle becoming established within Catholic Social Teaching.

In *Laborem Exercens*, an encyclical dedicated to the world of work, he places a special emphasis on unions of workers as vehicles of solidarity. He writes of the 'need for ever new movements of solidarity of the workers and with the workers'.[23] Later in the same encyclical he writes against a strong division of capital and labour to promote constructive order and solidarity: 'Both those who work and those who manage the means of production or who own them must in some way be united in this community.'[24] He goes further in *Centesimus Annus*, arguing that the defence of the weakest might sometimes place 'certain limits on the autonomy of the parties who determine working conditions'.[25]

In how many work places do each and every employer and employee know of each other's existence, let alone know of each other's lives? In many corporations and public bodies, those who do the lowest paid and most menial jobs are practically invisible to the executives and managers. These workers clean during unsocial hours, on little pay, often sub-contracted to an agency for the lowest price. Those whose office space relies on them may pay little or no attention to their working conditions, let alone their living conditions or their interests and concerns. This division of labour, common in many workplaces, is one example of a failure of solidarity.

The document within Catholic Social Teaching where solidarity is worked out in most depth is John Paul II's encyclical, *Sollicitudo Rei Socialis*. Here, John Paul II describes solidarity as 'a question of interdependence. When interdependence becomes recognized in this way, the correlative response as a moral and social attitude, as a "virtue", is solidarity.'[26]

John Paul II's concept of solidarity is demanding. It is 'not a feeling of vague compassion or shallow distress at the misfortunes of so many people, both near and far'.[27] Solidarity isn't occasionally giving to charity or simply being nice, but runs deeper than this: 'It is a firm and persevering determination to commit oneself to the Common Good; that is to say to the good of all and of each individual, because we are all really responsible for all.'[28]

Solidarity demands the members of each society 'recognize one another as persons', across social and other divides.[29] One of the reasons the low-paid cleaner of the high-paid executive represents a failure in solidarity is that the wealthier person may fail to see the cleaner as a person, because the wealthier person fails to see the cleaner *at all*.

John Paul II goes further, arguing that solidarity entails that those who are wealthy 'should feel responsible for the weaker and be ready to share with them all they possess'.[30] He preempts criticisms that this might lead to the less wealthy simply becoming passive recipients of the wealth of the rich. Solidarity also entails that the less well-off do not adopt 'a purely passive attitude . . . but should do all they can for the good of all'.[31]

In the example of the low-paid office cleaner, it's easy to see how the person whose office is cleaned might begin to view the cleaner instrumentally, simply as the means to a clean office. John Paul II's concept of solidarity 'helps us to see the "other" – whether a person, people or nation – not just as some kind of instrument, with a work capacity and physical strength to be exploited at low cost and then discarded when no longer useful'.[32] Instead of seeing the person cleaning our workplace as a means to an end, solidarity challenges us to ask how we might share the good things of life we enjoy with them and how they might 'be made a sharer, on a par with ourselves, in the banquet of life to which all are equally invited by God'.[33]

If solidarity demands that those less well-off are made sharers in the banquet of life on a par with ourselves, this has consequences for the way in which we live our lives. It also has consequences for the ways in which we interact with those less well-off than ourselves. First, in order to establish whether they are enjoying the banquet of life on a par with ourselves, we need to know those people around us. We need to build connections and relationships with all those in our community, not just those like us, or those with the same access to resources as us. Only then will we know how those less well-off than us might be made to share in the resources we have been entrusted. Only then will we know *who* in our communities and neighbourhoods are the less well-off, and not just in material terms.

The demands of solidarity, as set out by John Paul II, might mean that we are forced to make sacrifices for those less well-off around us: 'Solidarity demands a readiness to accept the sacrifices necessary for the good of the whole world community.'[34] Personally this might mean relinquishing some of the wealth and possessions that we have been entrusted, or giving our time or energy in a particular way. Internationally it might mean putting the long-term interest of another nation or community above the short-term interest of our own country. In policy terms, this would be a rejection of nationalistic slogans of 'our country first' which are gaining traction in many nations across the world. John Paul II's contribution to Catholic Social Teaching could be expressed as 'Solidarity first'.

The theological word for the sacrifices we might be asked to make as individuals and nations is 'love'. As John Paul notes, 'One's neighbour must therefore be loved, even if an enemy, with the same love with which the Lord loves him or her; and for that person's sake one must be ready for sacrifice.'[35]

Evangelium Vitae sees John Paul II returning to the principle of solidarity. In this encyclical, he unpacks the foundation of the principle, and grounds solidarity in the inviolable dignity of the human person we discussed above. Human dignity is the source of solidarity because 'the face of every person [is] a call to encounter, dialogue and solidarity'.[36]

He notes that all too often respect for 'the dignity of every individual and of solidarity between all people frequently proves to be illusory'.[37] He bemoans the tendency 'for people to refuse to accept responsibility for their brothers and sisters. Symptoms of this trend include the lack of solidarity towards society's weakest members – such as the elderly, the infirm, immigrants, children – and the indifference frequently found in relations between the world's peoples even when basic values such as survival, freedom and peace are involved.'[38]

We remember that *Evangelium Vitae* was written in 1995, and since then, in recent years, we have seen growing hostility and the demonization of refugee populations. Solidarity demands that the weakest in society do not become objects of fear or suspicion, but we accept the responsibility other members of the human race place on us simply by being human. John Paul II identifies the crime of those who fail to act in accordance with solidarity with the crime of Cain. Just as 'Cain does not wish to think about his brother and refuses to accept the responsibility which every person has towards others', so when people today 'refuse to accept responsibility for their brothers and sisters'.[39]

The *Compendium of Social Doctrine* offers a less radical version of the principle of solidarity than that set out by John Paul II. It notes that the term relates to 'the composite ties that unite men and social groups'.[40] However, it emphasizes more strongly than John Paul 'the space given to human freedom for common growth in which all share and in which they participate'.[41]

The *Compendium's* more modest understanding of the principle is reflected in its description of solidarity in action, 'the positive contribution of seeing that nothing is lacking in the common cause and also of seeking points of possible agreement where attitudes of separation and fragmentation prevail'.[42] However, there remains an element of self-sacrifice in the principle as found within the *Compendium*. Solidarity 'translates into the willingness to give oneself for the good of one's neighbour, beyond any individual or particular interest'.[43] The *Compendium* recognizes that for the principle of solidarity to be lived out more easily in our society requires a cultural shift. It calls for 'structures of solidarity' to be established to replace the 'structures of sin' that currently exist.[44] These structures will be the focus of Chapter 6 in our exploration of social sin.

We have already seen Pope Benedict's slight reticence towards the concept of solidarity before he was Pope Benedict, because of its origins outside of Christian thought. However, in the same address, he notes that solidarity entails recognizing 'that what we have been given never belongs to us for ourselves alone'.[45]

As Pope, his social encyclical *Caritas in Veritate* gives more space to the concept as he builds on the legacy of his predecessor. He notes that many people do not act in accordance with solidarity today, but 'would claim that they owe nothing to anyone, except to themselves. They are concerned only with their rights, and they often have great difficulty in taking responsibility for their own and other people's integral development.'[46] Instead, solidarity fosters 'first and foremost a sense of responsibility on the part of everyone with regard to everyone'.[47]

He repeatedly calls for a new way of thinking to overcome the increasing individualism of the modern world: 'A new trajectory of thinking is needed in order to arrive at a better understanding of the implications of our being one family.'[48]

Pope Francis reflects on the concept of solidarity in the light of social media and instantaneous communication. He is optimistic about such technology, which can offer 'greater possibilities for encounter and solidarity for everyone'.[49] He returns to radical roots of the principle as laid out by John Paul II which 'presumes the creation of a new mindset which thinks in terms of community and the priority of the life of all over the appropriation of goods by a few'.[50]

Like Benedict, he realizes that right thinking is essential to the exercise of solidarity. It stems from the recognition that 'the social function of property and the universal destination of goods are realities which come before private property', the universal destination of goods we encountered in the previous chapter.[51]

Francis is much more explicit that solidarity cannot be taken for granted but must be an active decision 'to restore to the poor what belongs to them'.[52]

Solidarity Forever

Solidarity, therefore, requires a constant effort on the part of the whole of humanity to remember that the goods and rights we enjoy come with corresponding duties and obligations. Foremost among these are the duties and obligations we have towards our fellow human beings. Without this active reflection on the impact each of our choices and actions has on the rest of the human family, we all too easily fall into the individualistic trap that the modern world pushes us towards.

One means of learning the reality of solidarity is by joining and celebrating some of the associations of solidarity which are the focus of the next chapter and the principle of subsidiarity. Beginning with the family, and moving into larger intermediary groupings such as workplaces, trade unions and voluntary associations, we come to realize our common humanity and how to practise the virtue of solidarity. The challenge we face is to make sure that we are aware of our solidarity with each and every human being, and not just those we like or who look like us. Our solidarity unites us even to those who are opposed to us, even to those who are our worst enemy.

The challenge solidarity poses is to remember that we are united even to those we find it difficult to relate to or remember. It reminds us that if we do not remember them, and our actions have harmful consequences for them even if we do not realize it, we are harming ourselves.

The whole concept of solidarity is best summed up, as Justin Welby notes, in a famous poem by John Donne. Given the biggest issue occupying contemporary British politics, it is a particularly apt reminder of the solidarity we share as human beings, and the obligations and responsibilities that solidarity brings:

> 'No man is an island,
> entire of itself;
> every man is a piece of the continent,
> a part of the main.
> If a clod be washed away by the sea,
> Europe is the less,
> as well as if a promontory were, as well as any manner of thy friends or of thine own were.
> Any man's death diminishes me,
> because I am involved in mankind;
> and therefore never send to know for whom the bell tolls;
> it tolls for thee.'[53]

Notes

1 *Evangelii Gaudium*, 188.

2 Rom. 12.5; 1 Cor. 12.12, 26–27; Eph. 3.6.

3 *Gaudium*, 38.

4 Ratzinger, J., 'Lecture to the Bishops' Conference of the Region of Campania in Benevento (Italy) on the Topic: "Eucharist, Communion and Solidarity"' (2 June 2002), available at: http://www.vatican.va/roman_curia/congregations/cfaith/documents/rc_con_cfaith_doc_20020602_ratzinger-eucharistic-congress_en.html (accessed 28 August 2018).

5 Leroux, P., *De l'Humanité* (Paris: 1845).

6 Ratzinger, '"Eucharist, Communion and Solidarity"'.

7 Wilde, L., *Global Solidarity* (Edinburgh: Edinburgh University Press, 2013), 21.

8 Welby, J., *Reimagining Britain: Foundations for Hope* (London: Bloomsbury, 2018), 39.

9 Suro, R. 'Pope Calls Solidarity a Rights Model' in *The New York Times* (12 June 1987), available at: https://www.nytimes.com/1987/06/12/world/pope-calls-solidarity-a-rights-model.html (accessed 28 August 2018). The homily can be found in Polish here: http://w2.vatican.va/content/john-paul-ii/pl/homilies/1987/documents/hf_jp-ii_hom_19870611_gente-mare.html (accessed 28 August 2018).

10 Pracz, E., 'John Paul II's contribution to the development of the Apostleship of the Sea' in *Polonia Sacra* 18 (2014), 95–107, 101.

11 *Centesimus*, 10.

12 *Centesimus*, 10; see also *Rerum*, 24; *Quadragesimo*, 88. Pius XI's articulation of the Common Good is the closest precursor to 'solidarity': 'only will true cooperation be possible for a single Common Good when the constituent parts of society deeply feel themselves members of one great family and children of the same Heavenly Father' (*Quadragesimo*, 137).

13 *Mater*, 23.

14 *Mater*, 157.

15 *Pacem*, 98.

16 *Gaudium*, 75.

17 *Populorum*, 17.

18 *Populorum*, 44.

19 *Populorum*, 62.

20 *Populorum*, 67.

21 *Octogesima*, 23.

22 *Octogesima*, 23.

23 *Laborem*, 8.

24 *Laborem*, 20.

25 *Centesimus*, 15.

26 *Sollicitudo*, 38.

27 *Sollicitudo*, 38.

28 *Sollicitudo*, 38.

29 *Sollicitudo*, 39.

30 *Sollicitudo*, 39.

31 *Sollicitudo*, 39.

32 *Sollicitudo*, 39.

33 *Sollicitudo*, 39.

34 *Sollicitudo*, 40.

35 *Sollicitudo*, 40.

36 *Evangelium*, 83.

37 *Evangelium*, 70.

38 *Evangelium*, 8.

39 *Evangelium*, 8.

40 *Compendium*, 194.

41 *Compendium*, 194.
42 *Compendium*, 194.
43 *Compendium*, 194.
44 *Compendium*, 193.
45 Ratzinger, '"Eucharist, Communion, Solidarity"'.
46 *Caritas*, 43.
47 *Caritas*, 38.
48 *Caritas*, 53.
49 *Evangelii Gaudium*, 87.
50 *Evangelii Gaudium*, 188.
51 *Evangelii Gaudium*, 188.
52 *Evangelii Gaudium*, 188.
53 Donne, J., 'Devotions Upon Emergent Occasions: Meditation XVII' (1624); Welby, *Reimagining*, 40.

5

Subsidiarity

'When I use a word,' Humpty Dumpty said, in rather a scornful tone, 'it means just what I choose it to mean – neither more nor less.'[1]

Subsidiarity is a term which has a range of meanings, even within Catholic Social Thought. Yet the *Compendium of Social Doctrine* lists the principle as 'among the most constant and characteristic directives of the Church's social doctrine'.[2]

Subsidiarity has also been adopted as a political concept, where it too is used by different groups, each understanding the term differently, even within the same document. Antonio Estella has noted 'the ambiguous character of subsidiarity. From a theoretical perspective, subsidiarity is so undefined that the concept amounts, at best, to a common sense principle of good government or a political objective. Subsidiarity therefore constitutes a very elastic notion.'[3]

Those who use the term in these varying ways are not quite as linguistically irresponsible as Humpty Dumpty, but it does mean that as we uncover the principle of subsidiarity, we have to explore a variety of understandings of the term. In this chapter we focus on the two main ways in which the term is used within Catholic Social Teaching, sometimes referred to as 'vertical' subsidiarity and 'horizontal' subsidiarity. However, even these qualifiers are used in different ways by different commentators, so caution is needed here too.

Of all the principles of Catholic Social Teaching, therefore, subsidiarity is perhaps the one that's most difficult to understand.

This is partly because the term is the most alien to us. At least, it's the term with which we are probably least familiar.

However, of all the principles of Catholic Social Teaching, it is also the one with which we come into contact most in our daily lives. This is particularly true for those of us who have ever lived within the European Union, where the principle of subsidiarity is written into the treaties which govern that institution. For countries within the European Union, subsidiarity is therefore a daily, if mostly unnoticed, reality. This understanding of subsidiarity is a helpful means to analyse how subsidiarity is being exercised politically. The political notion of subsidiarity is also a helpful way to understand the principle within Catholic Social Teaching.

The term was introduced into Catholic Social Teaching by Pius XI in *Quadragesimo Anno*: 'Every social activity ought of its very nature to furnish help to the members of the body social, and never destroy and absorb them. Therefore, those in power should be sure that the more perfectly a graduated order is kept among the various associations, in observance of the principle of "subsidiary function," the stronger social authority and effectiveness will be the happier and more prosperous the condition of the State.'[4]

In doing so, he built on themes unpacked by Leo XIII in *Rerum Novarum* concerning the importance of intermediary groups in society. For Pius XI, the principle of 'subsidiary function' is a means of securing social harmony and proper participation of individuals in society through these various associations.

In what follows, we first explore the principle of subsidiarity as it appears in political thought as a means to introduce the principle. We then look at the scriptural basis for subsidiarity, before turning to explore how different senses of the principles feature in the documents of Catholic Social Thought. We see how it differs from its political abstraction and how it relates to other principles of Catholic Social Teaching. Finally, we consider how subsidiarity might be applied practically today and the questions it poses for the kinds of nationalism that seem to be on the increase throughout the world.

Political Subsidiarity

In order to help us understand the term within Catholic Social Thought, we first turn to one of its political manifestations. Commentators often point to the seeds of the idea of subsidiarity in Aristotle's *Politics*, where the philosopher describes the growth of society from individual to family, to village, to city-state. He writes that 'the impulse to form a partnership of this kind is present in all men by nature'.[5] Subsidiarity is the ordering of society into different levels according to the size and influence of these groups.

The principle of subsidiarity has been incorporated into the political life of the European Union through the Treaty of Maastricht, signed in 1992. The Treaty saw the establishment of the European Union.[6]

For the Treaty to be agreed across the political diversity of the European Communities, it needed to balance the views of those who feared more centralization through an ever-closer union with those who wished to see closer integration between the countries of Europe.[7] Those who feared such integration included those who were sceptical of the European project, as well as those of regional governments, especially in Germany, who feared a loss of political influence at a local level. The principle of subsidiarity was decided upon as a means to balance these competing views.

It appears in the Treaty as follows:

- Decisions are taken as closely as possible to the citizen in accordance with the principle of subsidiarity.[8]
- In areas which do not fall within its exclusive competence, the Community shall take action, in accordance with the principle of subsidiarity, only if and in so far as the objectives of the proposed action cannot be sufficiently achieved by the Member States and can therefore, by reason of the scale or effects of the proposed action, be better achieved by the Community (Article 3B).[9]

Here we see two features of political subsidiarity. First, decisions are taken as close to the citizen as possible. In this understanding of subsidiarity, the citizen does not actually decide, but decisions are made as close to them as possible. Second, understanding is to do with competence of the higher-level organizations. This is a top-down understanding of subsidiarity. In this understanding, action is taken by the lower-level organizations unless the higher-level organizations are better placed to act on grounds of scale or effectiveness.

The principle of subsidiarity as it is found in the Treaty is vague, probably deliberately so in order to gain a wide acceptance across divergent viewpoints. There are no criteria given to suggest when a decision could or should be deferred up to a higher level, or down to a lower level 'closer' to the citizen. However, for our purposes, seeing the principle of subsidiarity in its political form introduces us to some features which find their basis in the Catholic notion of subsidiarity. These are proximity of decision and action to those who are affected by such decision or action. The second is to do with appropriateness of decision-making or action across different levels in a society.

The principle of subsidiarity as it has been interpreted politically helps us to understand the term. However, it does not exhaust our understanding of the term for two reasons. First, it is disconnected from the other principles of Catholic Social Teaching. Subsidiarity, perhaps more so than any other principle, relies on its relation with the other principles of Catholic Social Teaching. Second, it emphasizes only one aspect of the principle as we find it in Catholic Social Teaching; in this case, the 'vertical' aspect of relations between higher- and lower-level associations.

Margaret Archer and Pierpaolo Donati note how: 'Quite often, they (the principles of Catholic Social Teaching) are interpreted in ways which are very far from the meaning and intentions proper to the social doctrine. As a matter of fact, reductionist and biased interpretations prevail almost everywhere. For instance: . . . subsidiarity is defined as leaving decisions to the lower level of the political system.'[10] Andreas Føllesdal has noted other objections to the political use of subsidiarity 'deconfessionalized and shorn from its theological roots'.[11]

The political understanding of subsidiarity has introduced us to an understanding of the principle. We now move to see the seeds of the principle within Scripture and how it features in Catholic Social Thought.

Scriptural Basis

One of my favourite passages of Scripture is the account of Moses' judging in Exodus 18. The author is an acute observer of human behaviour, and Jethro, Moses' father-in-law, gives excellent advice about how to lead and organize effectively. Like many grandparents, Jethro finds himself looking after the grandchildren more than he might have chosen. (I sometimes imagine that he was probably looking forward to a quiet retirement.) In verse 6, he sends a message to Moses: '"This is your father-in-law Jethro. I am bringing your wife and her two sons to you."'

When Jethro arrives, he sees why Moses has no time to spend with his family. Every time the Israelites disagree about a course of action, they come to Moses for judgement to discern God's will on any given matter. '"You will surely wear yourself out, both you and these people with you. For the task is too heavy for you; you cannot do it alone"' (verse 18).

This is taking all of Moses' time, from morning until evening. Jethro advises the best way for Moses to organize the society of the people of Israel is by seeking out appropriate leaders to judge over different-sized groups, according to the competency of the leader. In this way, the people can decide minor cases themselves with the help of competent appropriate leadership at a lower level. Only cases that demand Moses' competency in judgement need to be heard by him. So, says

Jethro: '"It will be easier for you, and they will bear the burden with you"' (verse 22).

This is better for the people too, as their competency and judgement is improved through discerning appropriate action. Their homes are 'at peace'. It's better for Moses as he's less exhausted. It's better for Jethro too. The story ends with Moses letting his father-in-law depart and get back to what he was doing before the grandchildren so rudely interrupted.

The advice of Moses' father-in-law gives an example of subsidiarity in action. Moses is only involved in the judgement of those less competent than himself, when the issue demands it, and only when those seeking judgement are unhappy with the judgement of 'lower' judges. This both frees Moses to judge on those more difficult matters without exhaustion, and gives freedom and experience to those other judges to gain experience and develop competency.

This episode is the strongest scriptural basis for subsidiarity, but isn't the only pointed to by commentators. Albino Barrera, for example, highlights the relation between subsidiarity and self-sufficiency. He highlights St Paul's work ethic as an example of how 'people take responsibility for their own integral human development'.[12] He points to St Paul's repeated claim that he laboured so as to not place burdens on those among whom he ministered: 'You remember our labour and toil, brothers and sisters; we worked night and day, so that we might not burden any of you while we proclaimed to you the gospel of God' (1 Thess. 2.9).

Subsidiarity in Catholic Social Teaching

We have already indicated how subsidiarity is a term used with a range of meanings. We will now observe the range of meanings the term has within the documents of Catholic Social Thought and how the various meanings of subsidiarity are related.

The *Compendium of Social Doctrine* summarizes the Church's official social teaching. It presents the first example of how subsidiarity is understood in a different sense from those we've encountered so far, and how the principle is related to the inviolable dignity of the human person. The *Compendium* describes how '[it] is impossible to promote the dignity of the person without showing concern for the family, groups, associations, local territorial realities . . . to which people spontaneously give life and which make it possible for them to achieve effective social growth'.[13] It refers to these groups as 'civil society', which 'strengthens the social fabric and constitutes the basis of a true community of persons'.[14]

Such an understanding of competency is less to do with the appropriateness of decisions or action at various levels in the senses of subsidiarity we have encountered so far. The sense of subsidiarity hinted at in the *Compendium* is an example of 'horizontal' subsidiarity. It concerns the strength of intermediary social groupings, such as the family or trade union.

Subsidiarity in this sense has more in common with its etymology, being derived from 'subsidium', meaning to provide help or relief. Subsidiarity consists in a mutual relationship between the various groupings in society, each of which 'help' the others not only to exist but also to flourish. This is evident in Pope Pius XI's first use of the term, as we have seen: 'Every social activity ought of its very nature to furnish help to the members of the body social, and never destroy and absorb them.'[15]

This understanding of subsidiarity is 'horizontal' subsidiarity, which Alessandro Colombo notes is 'close in some ways to the original meaning of the term', while 'vertical' subsidiarity 'concerns the correct relationship between the various levels of sovereignty and institutional competence'.[16] Lester Salamon notes that political and secular notions of subsidiarity tend to emphasize 'vertical relationships between higher governmental authorities and lower ones', while the 'religious doctrine of subsidiarity focuses on horizontal relationships'.[17]

The principle as we find it within Catholic Social Thought is a good example of an understanding of the principle which emphasizes the horizontal societal aspect of the term. Subsidiarity is not simply a case of 'higher' or larger groupings in society, such as local or national government, avoiding interference in affairs of smaller groupings. Indeed, the opposite may be the case. Subsidiarity in this positive 'horizontal' sense concerns the flourishing of civil society and of the intermediary groupings which make up that society.

Subsidiarity might make demands of higher groupings to provide help and assistance to ensure that civil society survives and thrives. In *Mater et Magistra* the role John XIII ascribes to the State is hardly negative: 'Directing, stimulating, co-ordinating, supplying and integrating, its guiding principle must be the "principle of subsidiary function".'[18] Likewise, he argues that the State 'must facilitate the formation of intermediate groups, so that the social life of the people may become more fruitful and less constrained'.[19] John Paul II also notes that subsidiarity sometimes demands non-interference in smaller associations and groups, but also confers a duty of support, 'in case of need and help to coordinate its activity with the activities of the rest of society, always with a view to the Common Good'.[20]

The positive 'horizontal' sense, and negative 'vertical' sense, are spelled out in the *Compendium*: 'Subsidiarity, understood in the positive sense as economic, institutional or juridical assistance offered to lesser social entities, entails a corresponding series of negative implications that require the State to refrain from anything that would de facto restrict the existential space of the smaller essential cells of society.'[21]

Catholic commentators can also be found who stress the 'vertical' sense of subsidiarity, perhaps on the basis of other reasons for wishing to limit the size and scope of the State. For example, Michael Hickey frequently refers to subsidiarity in its vertical aspect: 'The principle of Subsidiarity, a central tenet of CST, states that government should be as small as possible and only as big as necessary.'[22] Likewise, Virgil Nemoianu, of the Catholic University of America, understands the term to limit the action of the State or supranational bodies to only that which *cannot* be done at any other level: 'If something can be done by the individual or by the family, it must not be pushed up toward a more complex level of society and assigned to such a "superior" level.'[23]

However, such an understanding of the principle removes the term from its basis within Catholic Social Thought. It is not that 'superior' levels, to use Nemoianu's term, cannot be involved. Indeed, subsidiarity suggests they should be involved – not to do that which can be done at a lower level, but to provide help for the lower levels of society to do that which they are able to do.

Participation is a keyword with which to understand the sense of subsidiarity in both its horizontal and vertical aspects. Participation is 'the characteristic implication of subsidiarity . . . by means of which the citizen . . . contributes to the cultural, economic, political and social life of the civil community to which he belongs'.[24] The principle of subsidiarity encourages the participation of everyone in society. It does so horizontally, in groups and associations which make up civil society, enabling the existence of such associations that enable the individual to participate more fully in society. It does so also vertically, both allowing the individual to take a full and active part in the decisions and deliberations which impact their lives, and through the growth of a democratic culture which is truly participatory and open to all in society.[25]

Subsidiarity, Civil Society and Associations

While subsidiarity is confirmed in Catholic Social Thought by Pius XI, the seeds of the principle were contained within *Rerum Novarum*. In this encyclical, Pope Leo XIII reminds us that the Church is not merely talking about intermediary associations in society as an abstract concern. The Church herself is one such intermediary: 'There is no intermediary more powerful than religion (whereof the Church is the interpreter and guardian) in drawing the rich and the working class together, by reminding each of its duties to the other.'[26]

The Church has an important role within society as perhaps the foremost institution for bridging social divides. At the altar there is no rich or poor, black or white, male or female but 'all are one in Christ Jesus' (Gal. 3.28). This description of the role of intermediaries and their contribution to the social fabric helps us to understand the role of associations within subsidiarity.

The community organizer Ernesto Cortes has written powerfully of the role of institutions in strengthening civic society, as a means of increasing democratic participation and the strengths of relationship within and across society. This is more important than ever given how long ago 'the alienating and homogenizing effects of globalization and the dominant market culture had begun to isolate people from one another and from their institutions, destroying our relationality and creating a new kind of tribalism'.[27] Recent elections, including the election of Trump in America, and Brexit within Britain, demonstrate the extent to which society is more divided and tribal than ever, and how pressing the need for a reinvigorated civil society which bridges these divides and acts as a buffer to prevailing forces seeking to undermine democratic participation.

Cortes notes the role that such institutions have 'in which we are taught the habits and practices requisite for a vibrant democratic culture. In addition, these institutions would have enabled us to develop the social knowledge to act effectively.'[28] Such institutions, he notes, foster the skills of listening and engagement with those of different points of view, and with different backgrounds, which rarely take place outside such institutions today. Think of how many social media feeds are echo chambers of friends and others who look like we do, think like we think, or support the causes we care about.

The role of institutions in strengthening the skills which make for strong relationship in society is thus a key part of the principle of subsidiarity. Cortes notes: 'Unfortunately people don't develop the capacity to have deliberative conversations on their own. These are skills that must be cultivated inside institutions.'[29] We see too why the principle of subsidiarity is important in allowing such institutions to flourish. The State and other powers have a duty according to subsidiarity to help cultivate these lower-level groupings, such as the church or mosque, trade union or youth centre. Without such support, hostile forces intervene to hollow out these institutions and the skills of participation which are sorely needed and which otherwise cannot be learned.

John XXIII, in *Mater et Magistra*, describes this role which such institutions have in 'the full development of human personality. . . the main vehicle of this social growth'.[30] He repeats this claim in *Pacem in Terris*, arguing that: 'Such groups and societies must be considered absolutely essential for the safeguarding of man's personal freedom and dignity.'[31]

The principle of subsidiarity elsewhere in Catholic Social Thought further explains the importance of such institutions. John Paul II notes that such 'intermediate communities exercise primary functions and give life to specific networks of solidarity. . . It is in interrelationships on many levels that a person lives, and that society becomes more "personalized".'[32] He also notes, like Cortes, the role such groups have in acting as a buffer for the individual who risks being 'suffocated between two poles represented by the State and the marketplace'.[33]

Two themes emerge as key within the institutions which make up this 'horizontal' subsidiarity: 'activity' and 'autonomy'. Intermediate institutions, as Cortes highlighted, are places of learning the skills needed to participate in society. Catholic Social Teaching also reminds us they are places in which human beings are able to act. They increase the potential for human action beyond the individual and enable activity which might otherwise be done on behalf of the individual by a larger organization or by the State. Such institutions are more 'human' because of their size, allowing each member to be 'treated as persons and encouraged to take an active part'.[34]

They are also places which respect and enhance the autonomy of the individual. Such institutions have an autonomy of their own, which enriches the autonomy of the individual.[35]

As Benedict XVI writes: 'Subsidiarity . . . is always designed to achieve their emancipation, because it fosters freedom and participation through assumption of responsibility.'[36]

It is for this reason that trade unions and similar associations, those intermediary groupings first praised in *Rerum Novarum*, are so important for the flourishing of society. They become the means by which the autonomy of the individual is promoted through responsibility and creative industry. Freedom develops this creativity and allows for the cultivation of good practice within a particular industry or region: 'The most important of all are workingmen's unions, for these virtually include all the rest. History attests what excellent results were brought about by the artificers' guilds of olden times. They were the means of affording not only many advantages to the workmen, but in no small degree of promoting the advancement of art, as numerous monuments remain to bear witness.'[37]

Subsidiarity in Practice

This creativity can be seen in practice by looking at one political example of subsidiarity. A regional government in Europe has adopted the principle of subsidiarity as a means to deliver public services. In recent years, the region of Lombardy has embraced subsidiarity through an innovative blend of governmental direction and local public and private collaboration.

There's not space to devote to unpacking the precise details of the arrangement here. Alessandro Colombo has edited an excellent set of review articles on how subsidiarity has altered the region's experience of political life.[38]

In that volume, Lester Salamon describes one impact of Lombardy embracing subsidiarity as an organizing principle: 'In the hands of Lombard authorities, the lexicon of subsidiarity has been deployed to move from state-centred to a society-centred approach to policy problems.'[39] He also notes that this has increased creativity through experimentation in the sense envisaged by Catholic Social Teaching: 'Decentralized structures foster experimentation by freeing local units from the often-deadening hand of highly centralized bureaucratic structures.'[40]

This has seen an increase in the activity and autonomy of various intermediary groups. There has been a greater sense of ownership of initiatives delivered by local groups, from childcare to healthcare provision. Through innovative use of public expenditure, local groups have been given the autonomy to deliver and design services. Here we see that the State neither simply scales back, nor simply delivers a service, but engages creatively to enable and support intermediary associations as those envisaged by subsidiarity within Catholic Social Teaching.

Benedict XVI highlighted the provision of public welfare services as one area of society where subsidiarity might be better applied. He relates it to the freedom and participation that subsidiarity is designed to foster through taking on responsibility, in this case for welfare provision at a local level.[41] He suggested that welfare systems created with active local participation might both improve services and save resources, through cutting waste, and eliminating fraudulent complaints, but also 'harnessing much dormant energy, for the benefit of solidarity between peoples'.[42]

He also suggests that 'fiscal subsidiarity' might be adopted 'allowing citizens to decide how to allocate a portion of the taxes they pay to the State'.[43] There is some evidence that direct involvement with how tax is spent through planning or hypothecation – choosing how tax is spent – makes the spending of tax on welfare and other social problems much more acceptable to those who do not benefit directly from that spending.

Making decisions about the tax spent on welfare provision or how these services are allocated at a local level both increases their effectiveness and the participation of the local community. Welfare ceases to be a matter for bureaucrats and becomes a concern for the whole community. If the local community feels that the system of welfare provision is in some sense 'theirs', either through the decisions to allocate funds in a certain way, or through co-delivering services according to the Lombardy model, this also decreases the risk that those in need of such welfare will be demonized as unfairly or falsely making claims on the wider society.

Michael Kitson helpfully summarizes why the example of Lombardy stands out as a good application of the principle of subsidiarity, as it is sensitive both to its vertical and horizontal aspects, 'as it [is] responsive to the needs of the local community and can ensure the best future direction for the local economy and the local community. The benefits of the approach is that vertical subsidiarity ensures that decisions are made at the lowest appropriate level and horizontal subsidiarity ensures that decisions are made at the nearest appropriate level.'[44]

Subsidiarity offers a means by which consensus might be achieved across society about how best to provide for each and every member. Pope Francis notes the importance of 'consensus building' in the pursuit of the Common Good at every level of society. 'The State', he writes, 'plays a fundamental role, one which cannot be delegated, in working for the integral development of all.'[45]

Subsidiarity helps the State, locally and nationally, play that role. It limits the risk that those who are in need of more support by society are demonized by those in need of less. In the current political climate, where nations such as Britain and America have revealed themselves to be bitterly divided, consensus building has never been more important. Subsidiarity, as proposed in Catholic Social Thought, and how it has been at work practically in Lombardy, offers a means by which welfare might be creatively provided without the demonization of those in receipt of welfare or social support.

Subsidarity and Nationalism

Division isn't only a feature of politics within countries in the contemporary political atmosphere. At the time of writing, we are seeing a return of nationalism to the mainstream of politics within nation states across the West. In America, President Trump is promising to 'Make America Great Again' by following a policy of 'America First'. In Britain, Prime Minister Theresa May promised a 'red, white and blue' Brexit (referring to the colours of the Union Flag), using her first party conference as Prime Minister to prioritize the national over the inter- or supra-national by declaring: 'If you believe you're a citizen of the world, you're a citizen of nowhere. You don't understand what the very word 'citizenship' means.'[46]

The principle of subsidiarity within Catholic Social Teaching provides an important corrective to such nationalism, grounded in the equal and inviolable dignity of each and every human being regardless of the lottery of birth. In *Pacem in Terris*, an encyclical devoted to good relations between nations, John XXII notes that: 'Mutual ties between States must be governed by truth. Truth calls for the elimination of every trace of racial discrimination, and the consequent recognition of the inviolable principle that all States are by nature equal in dignity.'[47] He notes further that so much has been done to 'nullify the distances separating peoples' and States should not act in such a way as to violate these reciprocal relations.[48]

John XXIII recognizes that the independence of nations is, even in 1963, increasingly a myth: 'Each country's social progress, order, security and peace are necessarily linked with the social progress, order, security and peace of every other country.'[49] In this context, he invokes the principle of subsidiarity.

We have already seen how, in a political context, the invocation of the principle of subsidiarity within the European Union served to balance the concerns of those who wanted closer integration with those who wanted to safeguard the decision-making power of the nation state.

John XXIII's invocation of the principle reveals a role for the nation state which transcends both petty nationalism and simple internationalism. He states: 'The same principle of subsidiarity which governs the relations between public authorities and individuals, families and intermediate societies in a single State, must also apply to the relations between the public authority of the world community and the public authorities of each political community.'[50]

As we have seen, subsidiarity within Catholic Social Teaching is not just 'vertical' or negative. Therefore, there is a role for communities at a national level, as long as they contribute to the flourishing of the human community. Moreover, in line with subsidiarity, trans- and inter-national roles do not simply step in where nation states lack competency to achieve a certain end. Rather, the role of trans- and inter-national organizations is also positive or 'horizontal' and demands that they actively contribute to the flourishing of the nation state as an intermediary community within the human family. This might displease those who want to argue strongly for the independence of nation states as they have historically emerged. Other nationalists might appreciate the support and continuing role given to the nation as an intermediary grouping. Those who wish to transcend geographical and national groupings altogether might therefore also be displeased.

However, John XXIII is also clear that the nation state is not sovereign above all else. Humanity always takes precedence over nationality. There are some problems he deems, 'which, because of their extreme gravity, vastness and urgency, must be considered too difficult for the rulers of individual States to solve with any degree of success'.[51]

Such international subsidiarity must also take into account the genuine flourishing of nations as an intermediary grouping, insofar as they contribute to the flourishing of the human family. Nation states, like all intermediary institutions, are examples of places where we learn the skills to participate in the wider human family. The human family transcends national boundaries: 'The fact that he is a citizen of a particular State does not deprive him of membership in the human family, nor of citizenship in that universal society, the common, worldwide fellowship of men.'[52]

Where subsidiarity demands trans- or inter-national action, it must never violate the flourishing and participation of intermediary nations with the human community. This is one problem with the manner in which political subsidiarity has been enacted within the European Union. In some quarters, it has been perceived as a means by which the European Union can achieve its will despite the wills of individual member nation-states. Gareth Davies notes that rephrasing subsidiarity within the European Union as a promise to 'make the maximum possible use of national authorities and bodies' to enact the will of the European Community would gain much less support than subsidiarity generally enjoys, even though it can be argued that this is how subsidiarity has functioned at a European level.[53]

Davies has also noted one reason that European subsidiarity has faltered is because of a lack of an agreed end by all levels of society, in which the principle of subsidiarity is applied. Contrastingly, Catholic subsidiarity supplies both the principle and the agreed end: 'Political power, which is the natural and necessary link for ensuring the cohesion of the social body, must have as its aim the achievement of the Common Good. While respecting the legitimate liberties of individuals, families and subsidiary groups, it acts in such a way as to create, effectively and for the well-being of all, the conditions required for attaining man's true and complete good.'[54]

Of all the principles of Catholic Social Teaching, subsidiarity is the one which is most difficult to subtract from the other principles, and from the wider body of Catholic Social Thought. We have already seen how it must be applied with an agreed end in mind. Moreover, for it to be applied 'vertically' without a detriment to organizations bigger or smaller in terms of influence, subsidiarity always presumes the principle of solidarity. As Leys notes: 'The principle of subsidiarity is the principle of competency to the principle of solidarity: subsidiarity presupposes solidarity. The first alone makes no sense; it can only exist within a society which is organized in solidarity.'[55] Without this, the associations and organizations of different size can have no confidence in how subsidiarity is being applied across the society as a whole. Lack of this confidence, due in part because of its abstraction from the other principles of Catholic Social Thought, has been another reason for subsidiarity faltering at a European level.

Returning to the question of nationalism in the light of subsidiarity, individual nations – according to the principle of subsidiarity as it exists within Catholic Social Teaching – cannot be instrumentalized to the end of a trans- or inter-national organization or corporation. Neither can nation states refuse international co-operation and pooling of sovereignty where it is clearly in the interests of the Common Good, both of the nations in question and the wider human family. Rather, the flourishing of both must be the means by which the principle is applied. As nationalism shows no immediate sign of abating within the West, it seems we are about to enter a period where the question of how humanity flourishes within and across national boundaries will be paramount. The principle of subsidiarity, as understood within Catholic Social Teaching, may never have been more important. As Nemoianu notes: 'It is on subsidiarity, I am convinced, that a truly serious and credible Christian Democratic thinking is and *has* to be founded.'[56]

Notes

1 Carroll, L., *Through the Looking-Glass, And What Alice Found There* (London: Macmillan, 1872), 124.

2 *Compendium*, 185.

3 Estella, A., *The EU Principle of Subsidiarity and Its Critique* (Oxford: Oxford University Press, 2002), 82.

4 *Quadragesimo*, 79–80.

5 Aristotle, *Politics*, 1252b–253a.

6 Council and Commission of European Communities, *Treaty on European Union* (Luxembourg: Office for Official Publications of the European Communities 1992), available at: https://europa.eu/european-union/sites/europaeu/files/docs/body/treaty_on_european_union_en.pdf (accessed 23 June 2016).

7 Lord Mackenzie-Stuart noted in 1991 that the principle of subsidiarity 'does seem to be providing at the moment a stimulus and bridge between conflicting views . . . not to put too fine a point on it, a little bit of fudging at the edges does no harm in order to reach the essential political compromise which is as the heart of that political animal,

the European Community'. Mackenzie-Stuart, Lord, 'Conclusions' in *Subsidiarity: The Challenge of Change* (Maastricht: European Institute of Public Administration, 1991), 160.

8 *Treaty on European Union*, 4.

9 *Treaty on European Union*, 13–14.

10 Archer, M. S. and Donati, P., (eds), *Pursuing the Common Good: How Solidarity and Subsidiarity Can Work Together* (Vatican: Pontifical Academy of Social Sciences, 2008).

11 Føllesdal, A., 'Survey Article: Subsidiarity' in *The Journal of Political Philosophy* 6.2 (June 1998), 190–212, 192.

12 Barrera, A., 'What does Catholic Social Thought Recommend?: The Economic Good as a Path to True Prosperity' in Finn, D. (ed.), *The True Wealth of Nations: Catholic Social Thought and Economic Life* (Oxford: Oxford University Press, 2010), 13–36, 22.

13 *Compendium*, 185.

14 *Compendium*, 185.

15 *Quadragesimo*, 79.

16 Colombo, A., 'Principle of Subsidiarity and Lombardy: Theoretical Background and Empirical Implementation' in Colombo, A. (ed.), *Subsidiarity Governance: Theoretical and Empirical Models* (New York: Palgrave Macmillan, 2012), 3–17, 6.

17 Salamon, L., 'Subsidiarity and the New Governance: Reflections on the Lombard Experience' in Colombo, *Subsidiarity*, 19–30, 22.

18 *Mater*, 53.

19 *Pacem*, 64.

20 *Centesimus*, 48.

21 *Compendium*, 186.

22 Hickey, M., *Catholic Social Teaching and Distributism: Toward a New Economy* (Plymouth: Hamilton Books, 2018), 19.

23 Nemoianu, V., *Postmodernism and Cultural Identities: Conflicts and Coexistence* (Washington, DC: Catholic University of America, 2010), 70.

24 *Compendium*, 189.

25 *Compendium*, 190–1.

26 *Rerum Novarum*, 19.

27 Cortes, E., 'Toward a Democratic Culture' in *The Kettering Review* (Spring 2006), 46–57, 46.

28 Cortes, 'Democratic', 46.

29 Cortes, 'Democratic', 47.

30 *Mater*, 65.

31 *Pacem*, 24.

32 *Centesimus*, 49.

33 *Centesimus*, 49.

34 *Laborem*, 14.

35 *Centesimus*, 13.

36 *Caritas*, 57.

37 *Rerum*, 49.

38 Colombo, *Subsidiarity*.

39 Salamon, L., 'Subsidiarity and the New Governance: Reflections on the Lombard Experience' in Colombo, *Subsidiarity*, 19–30, 20.

40 Salamon, 'Subsidiarity', 23.

41 *Caritas*, 57.

42 *Caritas*, 57.

43 *Caritas*, 57.

44 Kitson, M., 'Subsidiarity, Proximity and Innovation' in Colombo, *Subsidiarity*, 147–56.

45 *Evangelii Gaudium*, 240.

46 May, T., 'Full text: Theresa May's conference speech' (5 October 2016), available at: https://blogs.spectator.co.uk/2016/10/full-text-theresa-mays-conference-speech/ (accessed 8 June 2017).

47 *Pacem*, 86.

48 *Pacem*, 100. The dangers of 'economic nationalism' had also been warned against by Pius XI in *Quadragesimo Anno*, 109.

49 *Pacem*, 130.

50 *Pacem*, 140.

51 *Pacem*, 140.

52 *Pacem*, 25.

53 Davies, G., 'Subsidiarity as a Method of Policy Centralisation' in Broude, T. and Shany, Y. (eds), *The Shifting Allocation of Authority in International Law* (Oxford: Hart, 2008), 79–99, 99. The term 'arguable' is deliberate, as it is not clear to me that this is how subsidiarity has in fact functioned within the EU, even if this is how subsidiarity has been perceived or is argued to have functioned by some, wishing a stronger role for individual nation states. His argument that a mutually agreed 'end' is vital for any successful use of subsidiarity is a good one.

54 *Octogesima*, 56; cf. Centesimus 13 and 48: 'Always with a view to the Common Good'.

55 Leys, A., *Ecclesiological Impacts of the Principle of Subsidiarity* (Kampen, The Netherlands: Kok, 1995), 82.

56 Nemoianu, *Postmodernism*, 71.

6

Social Sin

We now turn to the first of two concepts within Catholic Social Teaching that arose originally within Liberation Theology. We shall briefly introduce Liberation Theology, and then turn to consider the concept of social sin which emerged within that theological movement.

What is Liberation Theology?

Liberation Theology is a theological movement originating in South America. Its basic theological challenge is the wider inclusion of the poor and marginalized in the life of the Church. Liberation Theology is the source of some key tenets of Catholic Social Teaching, including social sin and the option for the poor discussed below. Often these ideas are more radical in their original form within Liberation Theology, before they are assimilated into the body of Catholic Social Teaching, as we shall see is the case with social or structural sin.

Today, Liberation Theology is often understood to be defunct as many of its assertions have been countered and criticisms levelled against it, which some would take to render it obsolete. The thrust of these criticisms concerns the influence of Marxism and a narrow identification of salvation with socio-political liberation or improvement. This book is not a study of Liberation Theology, but it is important to note that while some pronouncements of individual liberation theologians might justify these criticisms, this does not mean that the insights of Liberation Theology as a whole can be discounted.[1] To do so on these grounds is premature. Rather, each thought must be evaluated in its own right, and its challenge heard by and within other theological systems.

It is important to distinguish Liberation Theology, as a socio-theological movement, from other theologies of emancipation with which it is sometimes grouped under the label 'theologies of liberation'.[2] The theologies which are grouped under this label are theologies which are rightly concerned with liberation of a variety of excluded groups on the lines of race, gender, sexuality, and so on. In this grouping, the poor (particularly the poor of South America) are understood to be the group which Liberation Theology is seeking to emancipate.

The grouping together of these theologies is often a move to lessen the individual impact of each of these theologies, including Liberation Theology. If viewed together, a criticism of one can be wrongly understood to be a criticism of all.

Alternatively, if viewed together, critics can reject all these theologians as partisan, regardless of their focus. Such critics can accuse all such 'theologies of liberation' at once of placing narrow self-interest or a particular identity politics ahead of the business of 'theology proper'. However, such criticisms fail to take the challenge of each of these theologies seriously. The uniting factor in all such 'theologies of liberation' is their challenge to conventional or traditional forms of theology to consider whether it too is partisan in favour of white, Western, male, established modes of thought.

For Leonardo Boff, such a grouping together of 'theologies of liberation' is indicative of a 'Central European perspective': 'Is the liberation of which this theology speaks a theoretical topic of urgent importance, to be examined along with other pertinent topics (work, sexuality, the demographic explosion) in the context of the present situation . . . Or is it above all else a historical process, a social phenomenon that touches the entire social and historical reality lived by the oppressed . . . for full liberation? . . . It is this point that distinguishes the Central European perspective from that characteristic of the Third World and of Latin America. The Central European study of liberation begins with the "topic" as such . . . The Latin American and Third World perspective starts from the opposite pole. First it examines the concrete experience of the oppressed.'[3]

It is therefore important to consider each 'theology of liberation' separately in order to ascertain the nature of its particular challenge to the theology of the Church. For our immediate purposes, this means considering Liberation Theology apart from other 'theologies of liberation' with which it is sometimes associated.

Viewing Liberation Theology apart from other 'theologies of liberation' also has other advantages. It means we can see that Liberation Theology is not only a particular historical movement within theology, but also a particular geographical one. It is not born out of the Central European mindset, but the Latin American perspective to which Boff has alerted us.

Alfred Hennelly finds a beginning of Liberation Theology in a talk given by Juan Segundo to students in Paris in 1962. In this talk, Segundo is reflecting on the peculiar Latin American context: 'Latin America is a context on the move. The speed of its movement can only be measured from within.'[4]

Segundo gave a similar address at a meeting of Latin American theologians which met at Petrópolis in Brazil in 1964, while the Second Vatican Council was ongoing. Roberto Maqeo reflected on the importance of this meeting to the development of Liberation Theology: 'The conference at Petrópolis had the aura of a beginning, a combination of conciliar language and a growing consciousness of the enormous task that still needed to be accomplished.'[5]

Maqeo alerts us to the importance of the Second Vatican Council as an inspiration for Liberation Theology. He also reflects on how this 'aura of a beginning' included the theologians of Latin America focusing on the peculiarity of the Latin American context for the first time. Before then, 'Latin American theologians were merely repeating the thought of the great masters of European theology.'[6] The meeting of theologians at Petrópolis resolved to 'awaken an active interest in theological faculties and professors of theology for exploring the horizons and clarifying the assumptions of research concerned with Latin America'.[7]

The spirit of the Second Vatican Council within the peculiar context of Latin America is what gives rise to Liberation Theology. This form of Liberation Theology is that which will go on to impact the nature of Catholic Social Thought.

Scriptural Basis

We now turn to consider the concept of social sin as we discover it within Scripture. In several places we encounter the notion of sin as a force which in some sense goes beyond the individual sinner who commits this or that sinful act.

In the Old Testament, we find whole communities and generations who turn together toward sin and away from God. In Judges 2 we read of the people of Israel, 'Whenever the LORD raised up judges for them, the LORD was with the judge, and he delivered them from the hand of their enemies all the days of the judge . . . But whenever the judge died, they would relapse and behave worse than their ancestors, following other gods, worshipping them and bowing down to them. They would not drop any of their practices or their stubborn ways' (Judg. 2.18–19). The idolatry of Israel isn't presented in individual terms but something upon which the whole community embarks.

Neil Ormerod notes likewise within some parts of the New Testament: 'Sin is not just an individual matter. It is a much larger social and cultural force, what Paul might mean when he speaks of 'thrones or dominions or rulers or powers (Col. 1.16; also Rom. 8.38).'[8]

We know of at least one sin within Christian theology that is reckoned to have a trans-personal effect. The sin of Adam, and its consequences, is not limited to Adam alone. As Paul writes, 'just as sin came into the world through one man' (Rom. 5.12) and again 'one man's trespass led to condemnation to all' (Rom. 5.18).

The importance for our purposes isn't that sin has effects beyond the sinner, as that is true of all sin. One of the reasons that sin is 'sin' is the consequences it has on others. All sin damages others, not least other members of the body of Christ who are also marred by the sin. As we saw with the principle of solidarity, if one member 'rejoices' all rejoice, so too if one member sins all are marred.

For our purposes, it is sufficient to note that Adam's sin maintains a sinful culture beyond his own sinning. His sin begins the cycle of sin, sometimes referred to as 'original sin'.

Just as with 'original sin', the concept of 'social sin' has proved controversial within the Church. We shall see why some are sceptical about the concept, and we will explore below the consequences to which they fear such a definition of sin may lead. Finally, we see how the concept was adopted in a modified form within the official social teaching of the Church, and in what ways it differs from its original articulation within Liberation Theology.

Unjust Structures and Social Sin in Latin America

We have seen how Liberation Theology came about in part through the desire to apply the spirit of the Second Vatican Council to the Church in Latin America.

The Latin American Conference of Bishops meeting at Medellín in Columbia in 1968 demonstrates this. The Conference produced a document whose English translation makes clear their debt to the Second Vatical Council and its spirit of *aggiornamento*, 'refreshing' or 'bringing up to date', that we described in our Introduction. The document produced at Medellín is entitled *The Church in the Present-Day Transformation of Latin America in Light of the Council.*[9]

The Bishops meeting at Medellín were also the first to use the concept that is the focus of this chapter. In their conference proceedings, the Bishops describe the potential for structures to be sinful. They decry 'the lack of solidarity which, on the individual and social levels, leads to the committing of serious sins, evident in the unjust structures which characterize the Latin American situation'.[10]

Throughout the document, the Bishops identify the role that structures play within the social misery and oppression that was common to the Latin American experience. Structures can, for example, be referred to as 'clearly unjust'.[11] A change in structures is highlighted, along with conversion of hearts, as an important ingredient in the recipe for peace on the continent.[12]

The document repeatedly describes how national and international structures must be reformed for the sake of the Latin American people. The nature of these structures is mostly left undefined, but includes governments, professional organizations and other associations. They are the intermediary groupings that we encountered in our exploration of subsidiarity.

The Bishops are also clear that structural change alone will not bring about social transformation: 'We will not have a new continent without new and reformed structures, but, above all, there will be no new continent without new people.'[13] However, the role that they ascribe to structures as a means of inflicting social ill demonstrates the beginnings of the concept of structures which have their own sinful agency.

In 1979, the Bishops' Conference would meet again at Puebla in Mexico. In a politically charged conference, divided between political conservatives and progressives, the Bishops go further than speaking of unjust structures alone and articulate the concept of 'social sin'. They describe the situation within Latin America 'as a scandal and a contradiction of what it means to be Christian, the increasing gap between rich and poor . . . in the people's pain and anxiety, the church discerns a situation of social sin, of a magnitude all the greater because it takes place in countries which call themselves Catholic and which have the capacity to change'.[14]

In doing so, they quote John Paul II, referring to the right of the exploited rural worker: 'He has the right to be rid of the barriers of exploitation . . . against which his best efforts of advancement are shattered.'[15] The Bishops meeting at Puebla see the 'barriers' to which John Paul II refers as an active force. It is by no means clear that this is how John Paul II understood the barriers to progress which the manual labourer encounters. Indeed, we shall see below that John Paul II will respond by defining the limits of social sin, stressing that any sinful social barrier was simply the result of the sinful actions of individuals in maintaining that barrier.

Medellín and Puebla are both official proceedings of meetings of Bishops from across Latin America. Like any ecclesial gathering, they represent a certain amount of compromise between the different perspectives of the participants.

We can see elsewhere within the writers traditionally associated with Liberation Theology the concept of 'social sin' inaugurated by Medellin's recognition of unjust structures, which Puebla articulated. Oscar Romero, Archbishop of San Salvador, writing in his second pastoral letter since becoming Archbishop in 1977, develops the concept of social sin as we find it in Liberation Theology. He notes how the Church has always recognized individual sin, but has 'begun to recall now something that, at the Church's beginning, was fundamental: social sin – the crystallization, in other words, of individuals' sins into permanent structures that keep sin in being, and make its force to be felt by the majority of the people'.[16] Clodovis Boff elucidates the concept further: 'Unjust structures or oppressors are objectively an evil. For this reason, they are "sin" in the material, structural sense.'[17]

Social sin within Liberation Theology, as we see it expressed by Archbishop Romero and others, is not just a collection of individuals sinning to maintain an unjust structure. It is a force which extends beyond them, the crystallization of others' sins into a structure that perpetuates further sin.

At first blush, such a concept strikes us as odd. However, a thought-experiment might help us to see something of the insight of Liberation Theology. Imagine an institution which is undeniably sinful, but not so evil that every action is obviously not in keeping with the Common Good. For example, a warehouse in a community with high unemployment, an hour outside a town and from the nearest shop, which refuses to allow its staff to bring their own lunch, and only allows an hour for their lunch break. The staff have no choice but to go hungry or eat in the vastly overpriced canteen, where a sandwich is more than an hour's pay. They dare not protest their treatment or bring in food for fear they might lose their job. We might describe the treatment of the staff as sinful.

The person responsible for establishing and maintaining such a working environment has obviously sinned, and is sinning. However, imagine the person responsible for establishing that sinful system leaves the institution, as do most of the staff with them over time. The rules regarding food and lunch hours remain the same.[18]

In a few years, nobody working in the warehouse will remember how it was before this system was in place. No individual will be responsible for the greed which is at the heart of the way our warehouse is run, and even if we convinced isolated individuals that things should change to prevent this system, it will take a persistent and substantial effort to make the system morally better as a whole.

Elsa Tamez notes how 'the sin visible in the system where ethical values are inverted, takes over all the inhabitants. That is why it is structural and therefore making all of us victims and complicit, large and small, rich and poor, so that it is not sufficient to convince isolated hearts that greed is not good.'[19]

Nobody questions this system which is detrimental to those in the warehouse, exploiting their hunger or forcing them to remain hungry. Those who enforce it will say they're simply doing what has always been done and are enforcing a neutral policy. Those who suffer under it won't ask for anything better because they don't imagine there might be another way.

Mathias Nebel reminds us of the experience of being in such institutions: 'Confronted with malign institutions, believing the fight already lost, humans tend to give up the struggle. This is to forget that the fight and the victory over sin, and specifically over structural sin, is not achieved by humans alone. The fight and the victory belong to Christ and humans can only ever participate in his fight and his victory, without ever being able to perceive its entire trajectory or its complete fulfilment. It is the loss of the theological virtue of hope which shows structural sin truly to be sin.'[20]

This is only one structure the workers' lives are impacted by. Many other such detrimental systems extend further to the whole community, the whole country, the whole continent and beyond. Many examples of 'social sin' are nationwide, those sinful structures that remain in place at the advantage of a small number of individuals, but which are impossible for the vast majority of us to think beyond.

The warehouse example is far from perfect, although it is almost certainly closer to, and less unbearable, than the unjust working conditions many find themselves locked into. It is an aid to explaining the concept of 'social sin' as the kind of pervasive, systemic sinfulness that sets in based on the actions of corrupt individuals but which somehow transcends them. Manuel Alcalá describes such sin as 'social when it goes beyond the individual and passes to the society'.[21]

Social Sin and Individual Sin

The reception of the concept of 'social sin' within the official teaching of the Church was initially suspect. One reason for this, as Daniel Finn notes, is that 'it is exceedingly difficult to present a rationally coherent explanation of social sin'.[22]

We now turn to consider the official reception of the concept of social sin. We will then see how the Church came to adopt some of the insights of Liberation Theology's analysis of sin within official Catholic Social Teaching.

Following the use of the concept by the Bishops meeting at Puebla in 1979, the concept of social sin was initially met with suspicion. Soon after, in 1984, John Paul II deals with the subject at length in an apostolic exhortation on reconciliation and penance, *Reconciliatio et Paenitentia*.

John Paul II rejects the notion of social sin as it is used within Liberation Theology and stresses throughout that sin is always the responsibility of an individual. He will not allow the thrust of Liberation Theology's concept of social sin 'in order to place the blame for individuals' sins on external factors such as structures, systems or other people'.[23] Instead, he insists that 'a situation – or likewise an institution, a structure, society itself – is not in itself the subject of moral acts'.[24] A structure cannot sin in itself, but only insofar as the structure is occupied and maintained by sinful people. We see this, he argues, because the changing of structures often does not end the misery of those impacted by the structure: 'The change in fact proves to be incomplete, of short duration and ultimately vain and ineffective – not to say counterproductive if the people directly or indirectly responsible for that situation are not converted.'[25] Social sin is only the multiplication of individuals' sins on a societal scale: 'It is a case of the very personal sins of those who cause or support evil or who exploit it.'[26]

John Paul II does allow for a more limited concept of social sin than that within Liberation Theology. He recognizes that every individual's sin is social 'insofar as and because it also has social repercussions'.[27] He also allows for the use of the term 'social sin' to describe certain kinds of sin, which are obviously anti-social. He gives examples of this class of sins, such as those which weaken relationships, deny human rights, inhibit another's freedom or go against the Common Good.[28]

He recognizes that the complexity of individual sins, when increased to a national or global scale, 'almost always become anonymous, just as their causes are complex and not always identifiable'.[29] In such situations, to which liberation theologians would apply the term social sin, John Paul II allows the use of the term, but only analogically. He will not allow 'sin' to be ascribed to the situation in the same way as it can be ascribed to the individual.

In this sense, John Paul II writing in *Reconciliatio et Paenitentia* gives us an example of those, described by Finn, who rejects the notion of social sin by arguing 'that sin requires a sinner, a conscious agent, and thus there is no social sin other than sin committed by individual persons, unless one uses the word "sin" analogically'.[30]

It is helpful for us to understand why John Paul II was so keen not to allow 'social sin' to be used in the sense it was coming to be used within Liberation Theology. John Paul II was not content with describing a structure as sinful. Instead, he insisted that there were individuals behind all structures whose immoral behaviour maintained the system. In short, he wanted to insist that in every situation an individual, or a group, is morally culpable. He feared 'social sin' leads 'to the watering down and almost the abolition of personal sin, with the recognition only of social guilt and responsibilities'.[31]

This condemnation of the concept of 'social sin' as intended within Liberation Theology is also founded in two documents which deal explicitly with the theological legitimacy of the movement. Joseph Ratzinger (later Pope Benedict XVI) as head of the Congregation for the Doctrine of the Faith was asked to explore the theological orthodoxy (from a Roman Catholic perspective) of Liberation Theology. Two documents produced by him condemn some aspects of Liberation Theology as reflecting too many external socio-political interests and having too narrow a conception of human salvation, namely the *Instruction on Certain Aspects of the Theology of Liberation* (1984) and the *Instruction on Christian Freedom and Liberation* (1986).[32]

In the first of these, Ratzinger shares John Paul II's concerns about removing responsibility for the individual. He writes: 'Structures, whether they are good or bad, are the result of man's actions and so are consequences more than causes. The root of evil, then, lies in free and responsible persons.'[33] All sinful structures are at some point the responsibility of the individuals who maintain them. To describe structures as sinful and to call for radical reform of them 'should not let us lose sight of the fact that the source of injustice is in the hearts of men'.[34]

His *Instruction on Christian Freedom* limits the use of 'social sin' to the same analogical sense we found in John Paul II. He allows for some structures to be described as sinful, but refuses to allow moral agency to be ascribed to the structure itself: 'For the sin which is at the root of unjust situations is . . . a voluntary act which has its source in the freedom of individuals. Only in a derived and secondary sense is it applicable to structures, and only in this sense can one speak of "social sin".'[35]

In some respects these official pronouncements and the insights of Liberation Theology are speaking past one another. John Paul II and Ratzinger's theological instincts prevent them from ascribing the action of sinning to anything other than an individual. This reminds us that in the midst of the most complex sinful situations there are individuals involved – individuals like us – who are responsible and must be held to account.

Liberation Theology, meanwhile, alerts us to the fact that sin on such a vast and endemic scale can often be self-perpetuating and seem to gather a life of its own. This is partly a matter of perspective. Ormerod reminds us that compared with traditional accounts of sin, which John Paul II and Ratzinger defend, 'the notion of social sin shifts our focus from the perpetrator of sin to the victim of sin. The poor are not poor because they have sinned; they are poor because they have been sinned against.'[36]

It will be important for us hold together both the emphases of Liberation Theology and those of the official response. We now move to see how a more substantial concept of social sin was adopted within Catholic Social Teaching, which charts a course somewhere between the two emphases we have explored in this section.

Structures of Sin within Catholic Social Teaching

The concept of social sin is incorporated into Catholic Social Teaching through the notion of 'structures of sin'. We shall see the use of this term is closer to the beginning of the evolution of the concept of social sin within Liberation Theology and the 'unjust structures' identified by the Bishops' meeting at Medellín in 1968.

Some commentators have identified precursors to the notion of 'structures of sin' within earlier Catholic Social Teaching. Daniel Daly finds the 'seeds for a social analysis of sin and its effects' within *Rerum Novarum*, particularly in Leo's understanding that the purpose of society is to promote virtue.[37] By implication, Daly reads Leo's critique of industrialized societies that do not promote virtue as effectively sinful.

Written during the Second Vatican Council, *Gaudium et Spes* provides the seeds for the identification of unjust structures, which we have seen was taken up by the Bishops at Medellín. We remember that Liberation Theology began as a movement seeking to apply the insights of the Council to Latin America, and was the purpose of the Bishops' meeting in Medellín. In some ways the debate over social sin we have traced is a debate over the interpretation of an important passage within *Gaudium et Spes*: 'When the structure of affairs is flawed by the consequences of sin, man, already born with a bent toward evil, finds there new inducements to sin, which cannot be overcome without strenuous efforts and the assistance of grace.'[38]

Medellín is not the only meeting of Bishops which makes use of the concept of unjust structures, inspired by the proceeding of the Council. In 1971, the World Synod of Catholic Bishops produced an important document, *Justice in the World*.[39] The Synod hears 'the cry of those who suffer violence and are oppressed by unjust systems and structures'.[40] It also goes further and recognizes the 'objective obstacles which social structures place in the way of conversion of hearts, or even of the realization of the ideal of charity'.[41] This is probably the closest official articulation of the concept of social sin as found within Liberation Theology.

However, the concept of social sin does not impact official Catholic Social Teaching until after it has been rejected in its liberation theological sense by John Paul II, as we saw above, and in the theological condemnations of the Congregation of the Doctrine of the Faith. This rejection of some aspects of Liberation Theology was met with hostility by those who felt it went too far in its condemnation.

It is in this context that John Paul II's next social encyclical, *Sollicitudo Rei Socialis* (On the Social Concern of the Church) was published in 1987. Having rejected some aspects of Liberation Theology, and its analysis of social sin in particular, John Paul II takes over from Liberation Theology some aspects of its analysis of sinful structures. He continues to resist the notion of 'social sin', but makes use of the concept of 'structures of sin', in a sense similar to that of the Bishops at Medellín.

The term appears in his analysis of the contemporary world, at a time when the world was still divided between communism and capitalism, before the Berlin Wall had fallen. He describes the world as 'divided into blocs, sustained by rigid ideologies, and in which instead of interdependence and solidarity different forms of imperialism hold sway'.[42] This world, he writes, 'can only be a world subject to structures of sin'.[43] He gives two concrete examples of structures of sin, 'the all-consuming desire for profit' and 'the thirst for power'.[44]

In introducing the concept of structural sin into Catholic Social Teaching, he refers back to his earlier rejection of 'social sin', and insists that '"structures of sin" . . . are rooted in personal sin, and thus always linked to the concrete acts of individuals who introduce these structures, consolidate them and make them difficult to remove'.[45] He goes beyond his earlier position and ascribes limited agency to these structures: 'They grow stronger, spread, and become the source of other sins, and so influence people's behaviour.'[46]

What explains this shift? John Paul II explains why he has given an increased, albeit limited, role to the agency of sinful structures: 'In order to point out the true nature of the evil which faces us with respect to the development of peoples: it is a question of a moral evil, the fruit of many sins which lead to "structures of sin".'[47] He recognizes the value in giving name to the sinfulness of structures and systems, in order to understand the nature of those systems as a means to overcome them. He notes that 'one cannot easily gain a profound understanding of the reality that confronts us unless we give a name to the root of the evils which afflict us'.[48]

He goes on to suggest means of overcoming such structures, 'a commitment to the good of one's neighbor with the readiness, in the gospel sense, to "lose oneself" for the sake of the other instead of exploiting him, and to "serve him" instead of oppressing him for one's own advantage'.[49]

Most importantly, for our purposes, is the recognition by John Paul II that sin gives rise to structures which themselves multiply and perpetuate sin, and these structures themselves must be overcome to stop the misery and oppression they cause: 'The principal obstacle to be overcome on the way to authentic liberation is sin and the structures produced by sin as it multiplies and spreads.'[50]

John Paul II repeats this notion in *Centesimus Annus*, recognizing again the importance of overcoming such structures and the difficulty of that task. The focus once again is on the sinful human decisions 'which create a human environment can give rise to specific structures of sin which impede the full realization of those who are in any way oppressed by them'.[51] The structures arise out of individuals' sin, but once again seem to have an impact beyond them.

The most extensive treatment of structures of sin within Catholic Social Teaching is found in John Paul II's *Evangelium Vitae*. Here we see just how far the later John Paul II had moved in relation to his original suspicion of such structures. In this encyclical, he recognizes that the responsibility of individuals can sometimes be lessened, and recognizes 'an even larger reality, which can be described as a veritable structure of sin. This reality is characterized by the emergence of a culture which denies solidarity and in many cases takes the form of a veritable "culture of death".'[52] His concern in the letter is primarily for those forms of unjust structure which lead directly to the taking of life: euthanasia, abortion and the death penalty. However, as we saw above in our discussion on the principle of human dignity, John Paul II also recognizes the attacks on human dignity which impede the development of the human worker through their exploitation or instrumentalization.

'Structures of sin' are therefore those systems which extend beyond individual actions to create an environment or culture which leads to further sinful acts, and brings about or sustains a situation of oppression and misery. They constitute 'an even larger reality' and present a duty to the Church to combat both the 'structure of sin' and the individuals behind and maintaining that structure.

More recent Catholic Social Teaching has made less use of the notion of 'structures of sin'. In part, this is due to the decline of Liberation Theology and in part due to persistent concerns about the need to ascribe the responsibility for sin to individuals. The *Compendium of Social Doctrine* notes the existence of such structures 'built and strengthened by numerous concrete acts of human selfishness'.[53] It reaffirms the place of individual sin within these structures, which 'are rooted in personal sin and, therefore, are always connected to concrete acts of the individuals who commit them, consolidate them and make it difficult to remove them'.[54] In many respects, the *Compendium* therefore presents a more conservative outlook with respect to the independent existence of these structures than the position of the later John Paul II. However, the *Compendium* remains clear of the moral duty to combat these structures wherever they are found.[55]

We have already encountered some of the thinking of Pope Benedict XVI on these structures through his instructions on Liberation Theology. It might not surprise us that such structures play little role in his contribution to Catholic Social Teaching. Daly argues that the concept 'has been functionally abandoned, but not rejected . . . Benedict has stunted the trajectory of papal thought that pointed to a moral analysis of impersonal social structures.'[56] Reference to 'structures of sin' is nowhere found in Benedict's social teaching, above a limited recognition of some structures leading to sinful social conditions.[57] For example, 'the structural causes of global economic dysfunction'.[58]

Coming from Latin America, we might think Pope Francis more likely to make use of the concept of 'structures of sin'.

However, it is nowhere explicitly referred to in his two social encyclicals. It is nowhere to be found in *Laudato Si'*.[59] In *Evangelii Gaudium*, he expresses suspicion that changing structures without changing the people within them will overcome the evil of misery and oppression: 'Changing structures without generating new convictions and attitudes will only ensure that those same structures will become, sooner or later, corrupt, oppressive and ineffectual.'[60]

In the same encyclical, he notes that: 'We can no longer trust in the unseen forces and the invisible hand of the market. Growth in justice requires more than economic growth, while presupposing such growth: it requires decisions, programmes, mechanisms and processes specifically geared to a better distribution of income.'[61] Pope Francis is much less interested in a somewhat academic analysis of whether a structure can be sinful. By using the language of 'unseen forces' and 'invisible hand of the market', he is alluding to the same social phenomena which were labelled within Liberation Theology as examples of social sin. He is more interested in the new 'decisions, programmes, mechanisms and processes' which are needed to better promote the Common Good and to safeguard human dignity.

Structures of Sin Today

Pope Francis' focus on what needs to be done, rather than what needs to be condemned, leads us to think about our own relation to social sin and the structures of sin today. His focus is an example of the seeds of a theology called for by Nebel: 'Christians should reflect: if unjust structures can be called structures of sin; if Christ's death and resurrection really overcame the sin of the world, then we should also expect and hope for a grace which overcomes these wicked realities. If structures of sin exist, structures of grace should also. Who will dare to write a theology of these?'[62]

Catholic Social Teaching has been clear, wherever it has touched upon the analysis of sin in society, that it is the duty of us all to overcome such networks of sin. This duty is an example of the theology of grace called for by Nebel, and which Pope Francis has begun to articulate within *Evangelii Gaudium* and *Laudato Si'*. This theology is not comfortable, but a courageous declaration of the truth of the Gospel to the systems and networks which currently organize society for their own benefit, rather than that of the Common Good and in recognition of the dignity of all human beings.

The duty we have to overcome such systems and networks that do not have as their basis the inviolable dignity of the human person is expressed throughout Catholic Social Teaching, as we have seen. John Paul II articulates this moral duty 'to destroy such structures and replace them with more authentic forms of living in community'.[63] He notes this 'is a task which demands courage and patience'.[64]

Likewise, the *Compendium of Social Doctrine* reflects on the increasing wealth of certain parts of the human family 'seen in the availability of goods and services'.[65] It reminds us of the moral demand of distribution of goods from rich to poor, stemming from the universal destination of goods for common use we encountered in Chapter 3 above. The *Compendium* encourages 'society as a whole to practice the essential virtue of solidarity'.[66] Those of us who allow structures of sin to cause misery to those of our brothers and sisters who are oppressed by them are failing to live out the call to solidarity as fellow members of the human family and children of the same heavenly Father.

We are reminded that we are to avoid becoming complicit in such structures of sin. Above all we are to avoid the sin of indifference, which is one of the greatest moral dangers we face. In a world of increasing convenience we are lured into indifference at the inconvenience and suffering of others which buys our convenience. We ignore the long and unsocial hours worked by those who ensure our supermarket shelves are stacked to the brim by the time we arrive at the supermarket each morning. We ignore the environmental damage caused by our addiction to packaging. We regard as little the labour of those who clean our offices and care for our sick or elderly relatives. We ignore the precarious and laborious existence of delivery and private car hire drivers, whom we want to beckon ever quicker and ever more cheaply to deliver us or our goods. We commit the sin of indifference.

A song from Pope Francis' native Argentina features in the recent film *Pope Francis: A Man of His Word* directed by Wim Winders.[67] The song is *Sólo le pido a Dios* by León Gieco.[68] It features as a refrain the prayer 'I only ask of God that I am not indifferent' to pain, injustice, battle, deceit, the future. This is a prayer for our time.

Notes

1 See Rowland, C., 'Introduction' in *The Cambridge Companion to Liberation Theology* (Cambridge: Cambridge University Press, 1999).

2 This is in contrast to those who oppose Liberation Theology being considered separately from other such theologies of liberation. See, for example, Joerg Rieger's review of *The Cambridge Companion to Liberation Theology* edited by Christopher Rowland in *Theology Today* 57.1, 145–7.

3 Boff, L., 'Vatican Instruction Reflects European Mind-Set (31 August 1984)' in Hennelly, A. T. (ed.), *Liberation Theology: A Documentary History* (New York: Orbis Books, 1990), 415–17.

4 Segundo, J., 'The Future of Christianity in Latin America (November 1962) in Hennelly, *Liberation Theology*, 29–37.

5 Maqeo, R., 'Meeting of Theologians at Petrópolis (March 1964)' in Hennelly, *Liberation Theology*, 43–7, 46–7.

6 Maqeo, 'Meeting', 43.

7 Maqeo, 'Meeting', 44.

8 Ormerod, N., *Creation, Grace and Redemption* (New York: Orbis Books, 2007), 52.

9 Second General Conference of Latin American Bishops, *The Church in the Present-Day Transformation of Latin America in Light of the Council* (Bogata: General Secretariat of CELAM 1970), excerpts available at: http://www.geraldschlabach.net/medellin-1968-excerpts/ (accessed 27 August 2018).

10 Second General Conference of Latin American Bishops, *Church in the Present-Day*, 'Justice', I:2.

11 Second General Conference of Latin American Bishops, *Church in the Present-Day*, 'Justice', II.19.

12 Second General Conference of Latin American Bishops, *Church in the Present-Day*, 'Peace', II.14b.

13 Second General Conference of Latin American Bishops, *Church in the Present-Day*, 'Justice', II.3.

14 Third General Conference of Latin American Bishops, 'Evangelization at Present and in the Future of Latin America', 2.28, translated in Eagleson, J. (ed.), *Puebla and Beyond* (New York: Orbis 1980) and in Spanish here: https://www.celam.org/documentos/Documento_Conclusivo_Puebla.pdf (accessed 28 August 2018).

15 John Paul II, 'Meeting with Mexican Indios (29 January 1979)', available at: https://w2.vatican.va/content/john-paul-ii/en/speeches/1979/january/documents/hf_jp-ii_spe_19790129_messico-cuilapan-indios.html (accessed 27 August 2018).

16 Romero, O., 'The Church, the Body of Christ in History Second Pastoral Letter of Archbishop Romero' (6 August 1977), available at: http://www.romerotrust.org.uk/sites/default/files/second%20pastoral%20letter.pdf (accessed 27 August 2018).

17 Boff, C., 'O Pecado Social' in *Revista Ecclesiastica Brasiliera* 40 (Dec 1980), 682, in Landon, M., 'The Social Presuppositions of Early Liberation Theology' in *Restoration Quarterly* 47.1 (2005), 13–14, 15.

18 Pope Francis makes the opposite but equally correct point that changing the system without changing the character of those who established or maintained such a system will also simply perpetuate the same sinfulness of structure: 'Changing structures without generating new convictions and attitudes will only ensure that those same structures will become, sooner or later, corrupt, oppressive and ineffectual' (*Evangelii Gaudum*, 189).

19 Tamez, E., 'Greed and Structural Sin' in *Trinity Seminary Review* 31.1 (January 2010), 7–15, 13.

20 Nebel, M., 'Transforming Unjust Structures: A Philosophical and Theological Perspective' in *Political Theology* 12.1 (2011), 118–43, 140.

21 Alcalá, M. 'Pecado Social Y Pecado Estrutural' in *Razon Y Fe* 112 (1985), 134, cited in Landon, 'Early Liberation', 16.

22 Finn, D., 'What is a Sinful Social Structure?' in *Theological Studies* 77.1 (2016), 136–64, 138.

23 John Paul II, *Reconciliatio et Paenitentia* (1984), 16, available at: http://w2.vatican.va/content/john-paul-ii/en/apost_exhortations/documents/hf_jp-ii_exh_02121984_reconciliatio-et-paenitentia.html (accessed 14 February 2018).

24 John Paul II, *Reconciliatio*, 16.

25 John Paul II, *Reconciliatio*, 16.

26 John Paul II, *Reconciliatio*, 16.

27 John Paul II, *Reconciliatio*, 15.

28 John Paul II, *Reconciliatio*, 16.

29 John Paul II, *Reconciliatio*, 16.

30 Finn, 'Structure', 137.

31 John Paul II, *Reconciliatio*, 16.

32 Ratzinger, J., *Instruction on Certain Aspects of the Theology of Liberation* (1984), available at: http://www.vatican.va/roman_curia/congregations/cfaith/documents/rc_con_cfaith_doc_19840806_theology-liberation_en.html (accessed 27 August 2018); and *Instruction on Christian Freedom and Liberation* (1986), available at: http://www.vatican.va/roman_curia/congregations/cfaith/documents/rc_con_cfaith_doc_19860322_freedom-liberation_en.html (accessed 27 August 2018).

33 Ratzinger, *Theology of Liberation*, IV.15.

34 Ratzinger, *Theology of Liberation*, XI.8.

35 Ratzinger, *On Christian Freedom*, 74.

36 Ormerod, *Creation*, 54.

37 Daly, D., 'Structures of Virtue and Vice' in *New Blackfriars* 92.1039 (May 2011), 341–57, 342; *Rerum*, 34.

38 *Gaudium*, 25.

39 World Synod of Catholic Bishops, *Justicia in Mundo* (1971), available at: https://www.cctwincities.org/wp-content/uploads/2015/10/Justicia-in-Mundo.pdf (accessed 28 August 2018).

40 *Justicia*, 5.

41 *Justicia*, 16.

42 *Sollicitudo*, 36.

43 *Sollicitudo*, 36.

44 *Sollicitudo*, 36.

45 *Sollicitudo*, 36.

46 *Sollicitudo*, 36.

47 *Sollicitudo*, 37.

48 *Sollicitudo*, 36.

49 *Sollicitudo*, 38.

50 *Sollicitudo*, 46.

51 *Centesimus*, 38.

52 *Evangelium*, 12.

53 *Compendium*, 332.

54 *Compendium*, 119.

55 *Compendium*, 332.

56 Daly, 'Structures', 352.

57 *Caritas*, 34: 'the Church's wisdom has always pointed to the presence of original sin in social conditions and the structure of society'. Elsewhere, he recognizes the role financial structures had to play in the havoc of the financial crisis (*Caritas*, 65). Overall he resists 'anonymous impersonal forces or structures independent of the human will' (*Caritas*, 42).

58 Benedict XVI, 'Address to the Diplomatic Corps' (8 January 2007), available at: http://w2.vatican.va/content/benedict-xvi/en/speeches/2007/january/documents/hf_ben-xvi_spe_20070108_diplomatic-corps.html (accessed 27 August 2018).

59 Shadle, M., 'Where is Structural Sin in Laudato Si'? (2 Nov 2015) offers a good discussion of its absence, available at: https://catholicmoraltheology.com/where-is-structural-sin-in-laudato-si/ (accessed 27 August 2018).

60 *Evangelii Gaudium*, 189.

61 *Evangelii Gaudium*, 204.

62 Nebel, 'Transforming', 143.

63 *Centisimus*, 38.

64 *Centisimus*, 38.

65 *Compendium*, 332.

66 *Compendium*, 332.

67 Winders, W., *Pope Francis: A Man of His Word* (Universal Studies, 2018) [Film].

68 Gieco, L., 'Sólo le pido a Dios' from the album IV LP (Argentina: Music Hall Records, 1978).

7

For the Poor

The regard for the poor isn't a surprising feature of Catholic Social Teaching. Almost all Christians recognize that God's concern for the poor is part and parcel of what it means to be Christian. It is found throughout the pages of Christian Scripture. The Old Testament contains instructions to remember the poor and the widow. The New Testament extends this ethic – the lowly are exalted by God's action in Christ as we hear in Mary's song, the Magnificat, while the rich are sent away empty (Luke 1.52).

The incarnation (God's being born among us as one of us) highlights God's commitment to the poor. In Christ, he takes on our poverty so that we might become rich in him (2 Cor. 8.9). Elsewhere in St Luke's Gospel, Jesus is clear: 'Blessed are you who are poor, for yours is the kingdom of God' (Luke 6.20).

However, this concern for the poor in Scripture is so widespread that we run the danger of overlooking the precise form of the concern for the poor in Catholic Social Teaching. The documents of the Catholic Church contain a particular form of social concern, which has become known as the 'preferential option for the poor'.

This chapter explores this important principle of Catholic Social Thought. We will explore what this preferential option for the poor means within the documents of the Catholic Church. We will look at the origin of the expression in the Church in South America within the climate of Liberation Theology and see how and to what extent the principle is understood differently within Catholic Social Teaching.

Finally, we will ask how we can apply this principle in our own context (whatever that may be). What does it mean to be a Church in which the poor have a 'preferential option'? What dangers are there in how we label 'the poor' and the marginalized? How can we as God's Church share his concern for those which human society deliberately excludes and overlooks?

Early Catholic Social Teaching

The preferential option for the poor is incorporated within Catholic Social Thought towards the end of the last century. It first appears in Pope John Paul II's encyclical *Sollicitudo Res Socialis* where we read about 'the option or love of preference for the poor. This is an option, or a special form of primacy in the exercise of Christian charity, to which the whole tradition of the Church bears witness. It affects the life of each Christian inasmuch as he or she seeks to imitate the life of Christ, but it applies equally to our social responsibilities and hence to our manner of living, and to the logical decisions to be made concerning the ownership and use of goods.'[1]

Before we go on to explore this principle in detail, it is important to remember that this was not the first mention of 'the poor' within Catholic Social Teaching.

Pope Leo XIII's *Rerum Novarum* is concerned mostly with the conditions of those in work. As such, the theme of poverty features as a backdrop to this focus on the conditions of labour. Poverty is a condition to be worked through: 'As for those who possess not the gifts of fortune, they are taught by the Church that in God's sight poverty is no disgrace, and that there is nothing to be ashamed of in earning their bread by labour.'[2]

Pope Leo spells out the Church's desire to see the poor 'rise above poverty and wretchedness, and better their condition in life'.[3] The role of the Church is limited to 'maintaining many associations which she knows to be efficient for the relief of poverty'.[4]

The writing of *Rerum Novarum* was in part occasioned by the growing threat of revolutionary change sweeping across Europe at the time. This colours the language *Rerum Novarum* uses regarding the poor. Pope Leo is not willing to suggest anything that might, as he suggests socialists do, encourage 'the poor man's envy of the rich'.[5] Instead, throughout *Rerum Novarum* he is keen to stress the common humanity of rich and poor alike. Both rich and poor are able to aspire to moral virtue.[6]

He notes, somewhat understatedly, that 'God himself seems to incline rather to those who suffer misfortune'.[7] God's preference for the poor is not yet taken as a model for our own attitude but serves 'to keep down the pride of the well-to-do and to give heart to the unfortunate; to move the former to be generous and the latter to be moderate in their desires' so that it is not difficult for 'rich and poor to join hands in friendly concord'.[8] This appeal for unity across divides of rich and poor is made throughout the encyclical. Elsewhere, the aid given to the poor by the rich is praised for 'drawing the classes more closely together'.[9]

The poor are signalled out for special treatment with respect to the preservation of their rights, and the State is seen as the means by which the poor might secure their protection: 'When there is question of defending the rights of individuals, the poor and badly off have a claim to especial consideration. The richer class have many ways of shielding themselves . . . whereas the mass of the poor have not resources of their own to fall back upon.'[10]

This language of 'rights' sounds strangely familiar to us today. It reminds us, as we saw in Chapter 2, of the importance of the thought of St Thomas Aquinas in the theological background to Catholic Social Teaching. As we have seen above, his definition of justice in his *Summa Theologica* understands justice as that which is owed to a person by right (or in Latin *ius*).[11] Catholic Social Teaching is steeped in this Thomist language of 'right' – not a modern understanding of human rights, but that which is owed to a person simply by virtue of being created by God.[12]

Rerum Novarum's treatment of the poor balances the universal demands of morality with the rights which the poor have as human beings. It attempts to alleviate the plight of the poor by appealing to the charity of the rich, yet sets out restrictions and limitations on wealth alongside the rights of each person. However, as the occasion of its writing demands, it is keen also to unite the rich and the poor together as fellow human beings, so as to avoid contributing to the revolutionary atmosphere of the time.

Forty years later, *Quadragesimo Anno* repeats the focus of *Rerum Novarum* on good relations between rich and poor, and advocates charity towards the less well-off.[13] Pope Pius XI begins the encyclical in purple prose which enshrines *Rerum Novarum* as the foundation of Catholic Social Thought. He describes the situation at the end of the nineteenth century as divided between those with abundant riches who 'wanted the whole care of the poor committed to charity alone' while workers 'carried away by the heat of evil counsel, were seeking the overturn of everything'.[14]

In these evocative opening paragraphs, Pope Leo's encyclical is understood as being written in response to 'unaccustomed numbers . . . begging him with one voice to point out, finally, the safe road to them'.[15]

For our purposes, *Quadragesimo Anno* restates this 'safe road' in its treatment of poverty. Importantly, Pope Pius repeats the role of the State as defender of the poor: 'The function of the rulers of the State, moreover, is to watch over the community and its parts, but in protecting private individuals in their rights, chief consideration ought to be given to the weak and the poor.'[16]

Once again, we see that the correct treatment of the poor stems from the preservation of their individually occurring rights. Charity is the primary means through which the alleviation of poverty occurs: 'It must always take a leading role.'[17]

Pope Pius builds on Leo's emphasis of the bond between rich and poor. This bond, strengthened by the leading role of charity, confirms rich and poor in 'the place in human society assigned to them by Divine Providence' by encouraging the rich to love the poor, and the poor worker to put 'aside every feeling of hatred or envy which promoters of social conflict so cunningly exploit'.[18]

If this social determinism alarms us, we find it reflected in the Anglican tradition too. In 1848 Cecil Alexander wrote a verse, now rarely sung, encouraging little children to become reconciled to their place in the social order: 'The rich man in his castle, the poor man at his gate, God made them high and lowly, and order their estate.'[19] All things bright and beautiful . . .

A final observation on 'the poor' in *Quadragesimo Anno* as compared to *Rerum Novarum.* The number of references to 'poverty' or 'the poor' decreases between the two encyclicals. This is certainly not because the plight of the poor was uniformly improved across the 40 years between their publication (especially when we remember the Great Depression happened in this period). Pope Pius suggests 'that the condition of the workers has been improved and made more equitable in the more civilized and wealth conditions' but also that outside such countries 'the number of the non-owning working poor has increased enormously and their groans cry to God from the earth'.[20] In this climate of limited social improvement and increased global impoverishment, the decline in frequency in reference to the poor is of note.

The theme of poverty in countries outside the industrialized West becomes dominant in the middle of the twentieth century. The theme of poverty takes on a global resonance, and the documents of Catholic Social Thought become increasingly focused on the duties of wealthier nations with respect to poorer ones. Pope John XXIII, on the eve of the Second Vatican Council, reflects this shift and makes it central to the self-understanding of the Church: 'In dealing with the underdeveloped countries, the Church presents herself as she is and as she wants to be – as the Church of all men and especially the Church of the poor.'[21]

In *Mater et Magistra* (1961), John XXIII insisted that financial aid given by wealthier nations must be 'disinterested'. It must be solely for the benefit of those poorer countries and not used to gain control over that nation or to further the wealthier nations' political standing. He writes: 'Necessity, therefore, and justice demand that all such technical and financial aid be given without thought of domination, but rather for the purpose of helping the less developed nations to achieve their own economic and social growth.'[22]

Pope John isn't only interested in the role of the State. He notes the part that individuals have within the State, however wealthy. In poor nations, he points to the role that individual Christians have within the economic and social development of their State.[23] In wealthier countries, he advocates a role for individuals. They are to help in training and increasing the efficiency of the development of poorer nations, as well as offering themselves to live and work in less wealthy areas. The Pope speaks with obvious pride in the role Christians have to play, describing those 'in every land who, in promoting genuine progress and civilization, are a living proof of the Church's perennial vitality'.[24]

This focus on the development of the nation state, repeated again by John XXIII in *Pacem in Terris* and the subject of Paul VI's *Populorum Progressio*, reflects the changes in global politics in the twentieth century. World leaders, the Vatican included, developed a keener sense of the dynamics between nations driven by the advance in technology and transportation, which has become known as 'globalization'. The Second Vatican Council, as a gathering of Bishops from across the world, is seen by many as the Church moving beyond its limited European viewpoint and confronting the challenges posed by this new global perspective.

This changing global landscape reminds us that Catholic Social Teaching is never static. It adapts itself to a changing world as it attempts to mediate the eternal truth contained within the Gospel. Nowhere is this more obvious than with respect to the poor. Pope Paul VI's *Octogesima Adveniens* illustrates the Church's awareness of the changing nature of poverty: 'The Church directs her attention to those new "poor" – the handicapped and the maladjusted, the old, different groups of those on the fringe of society, and so on – in order to recognize them, help them; defend their place and dignity in a society hardened by competition and the attraction of success.'[25]

When we think of poverty, we often think only of the financially poor, those who are economically marginalized. Paul VI reminds us to be alert to all forms of marginalization and impoverishment. He also reminds us to be alert to the changing nature of different marginalizations which serve to keep people in poverty, and the need for the adaptation of the message of the Gospel to these ever-changing conditions.

Paul VI had earlier hinted at this adaptability in his promulgation of the Second Vatican Council's 'Pastoral Constitution on the Church in the Modern World', *Gaudium et Spes*. This document is one of the most important in the history of the modern Church, reminding Christians that: 'The Church has always had the duty of scrutinizing the signs of the times and of interpreting them in the light of the Gospel.'[26]

The Constitution adds little to the earlier treatment of the poor in Catholic Social Teaching and mostly restates earlier themes from the encyclicals of John XXIII. It responds to its immediate context by noting the impact of the arms race between the superpowers embroiled in the Cold War as 'an utterly treacherous trap for humanity, and one which ensnares the poor to an intolerable degree'.[27]

It is important for our focus in this chapter as we see the importance which *Gaudium et Spes* places on the poor in the self-understanding of the Church. This gives us the first hint of what will become the 'preferential option for the poor'. The Constitution begins powerfully: 'The joys and the hopes, the griefs and the anxieties of the men of this age, especially those who are poor or in any way afflicted, these are the joys and hopes, the griefs and anxieties of the followers of Christ.'[28]

The Church's joy, hope, grief and anxiety is bound up with those of the whole human family, and especially those of the poorest in it. This singling out of the poor marks the beginning of the train of thought which will lead to them being given a 'preferential' place in Catholic social thinking.

The reception of the spirit of The Second Vatican Council in the context of South America would inspire the theological movement known as Liberation Theology. It is within Liberation Theology that the notion of a preferential option for the poor will originate. It is to that context we now turn.

Liberating Poverty

We have already said that the 'preferential option for the poor' originates in Liberation Theology. We now turn briefly to consider the option for the poor within Liberation Theology to discover the origins of the 'preferential option', before contrasting it with the option as it comes to be accepted within Catholic Social Teaching.

The preferential option for the poor is foundational for Liberation Theology. Norbert Lohfink describes it as 'the basic principle of Liberation Theology'. Gustavo Gutiérrez once noted: 'If one day someone posed the question, "What is the most important perspective in the theology of liberation?" I would reply that it is the Preferential Option for the Poor.'[29]

We must first note the sense of the term 'poor' here. Liberation Theology has been criticized for an over-reliance on Marxist theory. Liberation theologians Leonardo and Clodovis Boff resist this criticism, noting that 'the poor to which we refer is a collective, the common classes, which include much more than the proletariat studied by Karl Marx (it is a misunderstanding to identify the poor of Liberation Theology with the proletariat, as many critics do)'.[30] This wider sense includes exploited workers, the marginalized, bank workers, farm and seasonal labourers.

While the seeds were present for the preferential option for the poor at the conference of Medellín in 1968, it was first articulated in its full form by the Bishops meeting at Puebla in 1979, whom we encountered in our discussion of social sin in the chapter above. The Bishops noted the place of the poor within the Christian tradition, and committed themselves 'to make clear through our lives and attitudes that our preference is to evangelize and serve the poor'.[31] In a section devoted to 'the preferential option for the poor', they note that this 'represents the most notable tendency of religious life in Latin America'.[32]

It is important to note that the use of the concept at Puebla is more descriptive here than ideological. It reflects the Christian lived experience of the Bishops of Latin America. They note in the section dedicated to the 'preferential option for the poor' that it was an observable tendency within contemporary Latin America, because more and more religious are dedicating their lives to mission to the poorest in Latin American society. They draw attention to the consequences of this increased mission to the poor which has demanded solidarity with the poorest, and new methods of evangelization. They are clear that the option does not exclude anyone but gives preference and proximity to the poorest in society.[33]

If the term 'poor' is wider than those who are economically poor, or those deemed the proletariat by Marx, the term 'option' also has a different sense in Spanish than in translation. As Gutiérrez notes: 'In English, the word merely connotes a choice between two things. In Spanish, however, it evokes the sense of commitment. The option for the poor is not optional, but is incumbent upon every Christian. It is not something that a Christian can either take or leave.'[34] It might be better translated as the preferential *obligation* for the poor.

Elsewhere Gutiérrez notes that preferential option for the poor is not only an obligation for the non-poor, but 'a decision incumbent upon every Christian'.[35] He notes that the poor have to decide against all of the forms of poverty and marginalization which society inflicts, 'to opt in favour of their sisters and brothers by race, social class and culture'.[36]

The preferential option for the poor therefore goes further than just the traditional focus of Christian charity. As Ormerod notes: 'The option for the poor has two aspects, one practical and the other hermeneutical. The practical aspect is that the poor have the first call on the resources of the world . . . The hermeneutical aspect relates to the privileged position of the poor in grasping the nature of social reality.'[37]

Finally, we should note that the preferential option for the poor is not only to do with our relations to each other, that is, how the non-poor treat the poor. It does not only derive from the observation of contemporary Latin American evangelical efforts. Rather, it derives from Latin American reflection on the nature and character of God.

Gutiérrez highlights repeatedly that the preferential option for the poor derives from God's own revelation as being on the side of the poor: 'The ultimate basis of God's preference for the poor is to be found in God's own goodness and not in any analysis of society of human compassion, however pertinent these reasons may be.'[38] Elsewhere he notes: 'We should prefer them [the poor] not because they are good (if they are, fine!) but because first of all God is good and prefers the forgotten, the oppressed, the poor, the abandoned.'[39]

The Preferential Option for the Poor

The first social encyclical to be written after the impact of Liberation Theology is John Paul II's *Laborem Exercens* in 1981. It is produced as the hierarchy of the Church sought to discern the extent to which Liberation Theology was a result of the promptings of the Spirit. At one level, the whole encyclical deals with the poverty, as it is addressed to the importance and dignity of work and just working conditions. The poor are mentioned explicitly only on three occasions, but they play a significant role in John Paul II's vision of the Church. He calls for the Church to be a 'Church of the poor'.[40] He builds on Paul VI's recognition of the many kinds of poverty as 'the "poor" appear under various forms'.[41] While he is not more explicit on the kinds of poverty, he unpacks the concrete causes of poverty, 'the scourge of unemployment' and the low value 'put on work and the rights that flow from it, especially the right to a just wage and to the personal security of the worker and his or her family'.[42]

Sollicitudo Rei Socialis, written by John Paul II, is the first explicit inclusion of the preferential option for the poor within Catholic Social Teaching. Written in 1987, it is published following the debate that arose as a result of the Congregation of the Doctrine of the Faith's condemnation of some aspects of Liberation Theology.

In this context, John Paul II takes over the preferential option of the poor. He defines it as 'a special form of primacy in the exercise of Christian charity, to which the whole tradition of the Church bears witness'.[43] He outlines the concrete meaning of the preferential option for the poor in the life of the Christian: 'It applies equally to our social responsibilities and hence to our manner of living, and to the logical decisions to be made concerning the ownership and use of goods.'[44] This is not simply a nod to the poor, but a decisive call to action, which 'must be translated at all levels into concrete actions, until it decisively attains a series of necessary reforms'.[45]

This concern for poverty, which should be a prime basis for our manner of living the Christian life, is not limited to those experiencing material poverty, as John Paul II reminds us: 'One must not overlook that special form of poverty which consists in being deprived of fundamental human rights.'[46]

In *Centesimus Annus*, written on the 100th anniversary of *Rerum Novarum*, John Paul II once again sets out the preferential option for the poor. In this encyclical, he sees *Rerum Novarum* as an early example of the Church's support for the principle.[47] However, he interprets the principle in such a way as to rob it of some of its force, as he defines it as 'never exclusive or discriminatory towards other groups'.[48] It is true that Christian action and proclamation are not limited to the poor alone, but some of the force of the preferential option for the poor is that it discriminates towards the poor in a world in which cycles of poverty can be almost impossible to overcome. John Paul II repeats the breadth of poverty that is included under the banner of the 'poor' which includes economic, cultural and spiritual poverty, especially the poverty of economic migrants and refugees.[49] He highlights throughout the encyclical the contribution of inequality between rich and poor nations to the continued poverty of the developing world.[50]

His most significant contribution to the option for the poor in this encyclical is the call 'to abandon a mentality in which the poor – as individuals and as peoples – are considered a burden, as irksome intruders trying to consume what others have produced'.[51] This recognizes that the call of the poor for equal access to resources is not just a call for similar access to a level of resources equivalent to those we currently enjoy, but a call for a share of the resources we are currently stewarding badly. The call of the poor is thus a reminder against our profligate use of resources that they have a rightful share in, because of the Common Good and the universal destination of goods for common use we have already explored in Chapter 3 above.

It is precisely in the context of the universal destination of goods that the preferential option for the poor is included in the *Compendium of Social Doctrine*. The language of the *Compendium* is clear: 'The principle of the universal destination of goods requires that the poor, the marginalized and in all cases those whose living conditions interfere with their proper growth should be the focus of particular concern. To this end, the preferential option for the poor should be reaffirmed in all its force.'[52] The combination of the preference for the poor with the universal destination of goods challenges us to ask if we are using the resources at our disposal with a view to the Common Good and the good of the poor in particular.

Benedict XVI reaffirms the Church's commitment to the poor, and especially to the poor within the so-called 'developing world'. He draws attention to the inequality between rich and poor and between rich and poor nations. In particular, he highlights the growing separation of the rich and poor: 'While the poor of the world continue knocking on the doors of the rich, the world of affluence runs the risk of no longer hearing those knocks, on account of a conscience that can no longer distinguish what is human.'[53] He calls for a cultivation of awareness and conscience on the part of the rich so that we are not deaf to the cries of the poor.

Benedict XVI also moves the preferential option of the poor beyond mere charity. In so doing he deepens the theological basis of the preferential option for the poor through reflection on the incarnation: 'The preferential option for the poor is implicit in the Christological faith in the God who became poor for us, so as to enrich us with his poverty.'[54] We have seen here that he is building on the theological development of the preference within Liberation Theology, and its reflection on the nature of God who sides with the poor of humanity.

Following Benedict, Pope Francis' whole pontificate has been directed towards the poor. His choice of the name Francis is an indication of this priority within his papacy. St Francis of Assisi established a band of poor brothers, living a life of evangelical poverty with and for the poor of his day. Pope Francis has made important symbolic demonstrations of this commitment to poverty, shunning large papal apartments and limousines. It is therefore no surprise that we find the preferential option for the poor to be a focus of both his existing contributions to Catholic Social Teaching.

His apostolic exhortation *Evangelii Gaudium* refers to the preferential option for the poor repeatedly. He finds a scriptural basis for the option in Galatians 2.10, suggesting 'the key criterion of the authenticity which [the Apostles] presented was that he should not forget the poor'.[55] Pope Francis identifies the option for the poor as an essential component to all proclamation of the Gospel: 'There is one sign which we should never lack: the option for those who are least, those whom society discards.'[56] This emphasis on the indispensability of the option for the poor is challenging as it shames those evangelistic endeavours orientated primarily or solely towards the wealthy or middle classes, which are often those regarded as most successful by ecclesial authorities as they appear so in worldly terms.

Pope Francis develops Benedict's theological analysis of the option for the poor: 'For the option for the poor is primarily a theological category rather than a cultural, sociological, political or philosophical one.'[57] The preferential option for the poor has implications for the manner in which we proceed theologically. Francis continues: 'This is why I want a Church which is poor and for the poor . . . we need to let ourselves be evangelized by them.'[58] Francis adds the 'hermeneutical aspect' of the option for the poor, referred to by Ormerod, to the Church's teaching, which 'relates to the privileged position of the poor in grasping the nature of social reality'.[59] Through their closeness to Christ in suffering, the poor reveal Christ in a way that the rich do not in their wealth, and we must be transformed by Christ in them.

Francis reiterates the preferential option for the poor in *Laudato Si'*. Here it is linked to the Common Good, and Francis follows the *Compendium* in linking the preferential option to the universal destination of goods.[60] The whole encyclical is a hymn against poverty and a call for justice between nations, and across the planet in terms of our distribution and use of shared resources. We are reminded once again that the option for the poor is not optional, but a demand of Christian duty: 'This option is in fact an ethical imperative essential for effectively attaining the Common Good.'[61]

A Church for the Poor

We have considered the preference for the poor throughout its history within Liberation Theology and Catholic Social Teaching. We move now to consider what this preference means for the Christian life and the way in which we organize our church communities.

The widespread evidence for God's concern for the poor in Scripture means that the Catholic Church is not the only church to reflect on the option for the poor. Other denominations, which do not have the direct influence of Liberation Theology, may prefer other forms of language for this preference, but this concern is widespread.

We see an example of this within the Church of England's intervention in the build-up to the 2015 General Election. The House of Bishops of the Church of England published an open letter entitled 'Who is My Neighbour?' They reflect on the apparent contrast between our society's presumption of equality as a principle across humankind and the realities of how people are spoken of within that same society: 'Most people, when asked, subscribe to some version of the idea that all people are created equal. Yet this is contradicted in the way that some categories of people are spoken about – people who are sick, disabled, terminally ill or otherwise unable to live the life that a consumer society celebrates; people who are unable to work, materially poor or mentally ill in ways which challenge "acceptable" ways of being unwell. There is a deep contradiction in the attitudes of a society which celebrates equality in principle yet treats some people, especially the poor and vulnerable, as unwanted, unvalued and unnoticed.'[62]

This is not the only intervention on the part of the Church of England hierarchy in the run-up to an election. The Archbishops of York and Canterbury also wrote to the parishes and chaplaincies of the Church of England ahead of the 2017 General Election. In this letter, the poor are referred to twice. First, in reference to the Common Good: 'The United Kingdom, when at its best, has been represented by a sense not only of living for ourselves, but by a deeper concern for the weak, poor and marginalized, and for the Common Good.'[63]

The second reference to the poor in the Archbishops' letter is in relation to education. They highlight the importance of education as a means for overcoming divides between rich and poor, 'tackling with vigour the exclusion of the poorest groups from future economic life'.[64]

These two interventions have been chosen as they demonstrate a recent trend within the life of a significant Christian denomination. First, we note references to 'the poor' have decreased. 'Who is My Neighbour?' refers to the poor six times in 2015, compared to the two mentions of the poor in 2017. Second, we note a restriction of audience – from an open letter in 2015, to 2017. At a senior level, the Church of England seems to be losing confidence in speaking into the public sphere on this issue of poverty.

In this environment, an address by the Bishop of Burnley, Philip North, in the summer of 2017 is significant. Bishop North spoke at the gathering of Christian leaders known as New Wine and challenged the Church on precisely this trend, and an apparent lack of interest in the poor and the outcast.

Bishop North has suggested that the trend of decreasing interest in the poor is not unusual within recent years. Rather it is reflective of a pattern within the Church to reduce our focus on, and ministry alongside, the so-called 'poor'. He provocatively suggests further that this is the reason behind Church decline that all denominations have experienced in recent decades. Bishop North claims the reasons behind the acceleration of the decline are 'straightforward . . . It's because we've forgotten the poor.'

If this is true, it is not only the Church. The shocking events at Grenfell Tower in the summer of 2017, in which 71 individuals died in a fire in a tower-block which included a large number of social tenants, brought to the attention of the nation at large that there are large sections of society which are 'unwanted, unvalued and unnoticed'. These include the economically and materially poor.

The events of Grenfell Tower were particularly shocking because of the suggestions that the safety of the economically and materially poor tenants was put at risk by the council for the benefit of more economically advantaged local residents who objected to the building's appearance. Rather than place the poor in a place of preference, it seemed that the voices of the poor were overlooked.

We might now apply the insight of Catholic Social Teaching that the poor ought to have a preferential place in the life of the Church and in our decision-making. Bishop North has suggested that this does not happen at present. Rather, the poor are overlooked in current Church practice, as well as across society at large.

We can remind ourselves of the form of primacy which Catholic Social Teaching has adopted, 'a special form of primacy in the exercise of Christian charity, to which the whole tradition of the Church bears witness. It affects the life of each Christian inasmuch as he or she seeks to imitate the life of Christ, but it applies equally to our social responsibilities and hence to our manner of living, and to the logical decisions to be made concerning the ownership and use of goods . . . this love of preference for the poor, and the decisions which it inspires in us, cannot but embrace the immense multitudes of . . . those without hope of a better future. It is impossible not to take account of the existence of these realities. To ignore them would mean becoming like the "rich man" who pretended not to know the beggar Lazarus lying at his gate.'[65]

We should ensure that we are sharing God's preference for the marginalized and the overlooked in our proclamation of the Gospel. The first step in doing so is to make sure *all* of our decisions consider the poor and marginalized within our contexts as part of our decision-making processes.

Further, all our decisions should be made with an awareness of their impact on the poor and the marginalized first. This consideration should be one of the most important in deciding which course of action to take. Considering the impact of decisions on the poor first would be to adopt the insight that the poor not only have an option within our churches and communities, but a *preferential* place.

Danger: Language Matters

This is, however, hazardous territory if we are to avoid our ministry participating in, and at worst furthering, the patterns of marginalization which have led to the economic and material poverty many experience as a living reality.

The remainder of this chapter serves to highlight further potential dangers we hope any focus on 'the poor' would intentionally seek to avoid as a means to overcome both the conditions and causes of poverty. It is important to remember the insight from Catholic Social Teaching we saw above that there are different kinds of poverty. The varying Beatitudes of

Matthew and Luke remind us that there is material as well as spiritual poverty. For the remainder of this chapter, we shall be focusing on those people who are economically marginalized.

Bishop North's address at the New Wine conference in 2017 closed by suggesting, 'for when we speak hope to the poor, we speak hope to everyone'. There are dangers here. We must be careful about speaking 'to' the poor, if we are truly to adopt the insight of Catholic Social Teaching that the poor have a preferential place.

When the economically impoverished are 'spoken to' or 'at', rather than *listened to*, a power dynamic is maintained which is reflective of that same dynamic at work in society which is at the root of such poverty. Rather than the poor being given a preferential place as sources of insight, those of us who have something speak *at* those of us without. Instead, to recognize their preferential place, we must listen to what God is saying already to 'the poor' by listening to them. We trust that not only we have something to say to the poor, but that God might already be speaking to them and through them.

In saying this, we are alerted to another danger. It is all too easy to make our ministry to the poor about *us* and what they can teach *us* as economically better-off about the life of faith. It is all too easy to say that God has privileged the poor by speaking to them; we must listen to them, and they have something to share with us. Pope Francis veers close to this: 'This is why I want a Church which is poor and for the poor. They have much to teach us.'[66]

This might be true, but it runs the risk of instrumentalizing the economically marginalized for our spiritual benefit. It denies the poor their preferential place. Our ministry must always seek to end the processes of marginalization which are contrary to Christ's will, and harm fellow members and potential members of his Body. Instead of being intent on learning from the economically marginalized, we must listen to them.

Listening only goes so far. A ministry which recognizes the preferential option for the poor will want to alleviate the symptoms of poverty. However, we run into another danger here. If our ministry stops at service provision or poverty relief, we may further entrench the patterns which gave rise to economic impoverishment in the first place. Food banks and soup kitchens play an important role in alleviating immediate need, but they must go hand in hand with efforts to address the underlying causes of such poverty. If not, the presence of food banks and soup kitchens can vaccinate us against the horror of poverty. Instead of focusing our efforts on alleviating the cause of poverty, we instead further the process of impoverishment by placing a sticking plaster over the causes of poverty in the first place. To recognize the preferential option of the poor means we go beyond *compassion*, and seek *justice*. This will be a primary aim of our ministry in this area, so that those currently in poverty might share more in the economic benefits that society at large might enjoy.

Language matters. Just as there are dangers in 'speaking to' or 'at' 'the poor', so there are dangers in being Church *for* them. In his address, Bishop North used the phrase 'Church for the poor' six times. His examples of previous successful evangelical efforts are often forms of service provision similar to those described above (food banks and soup kitchens) alongside missionary work. While Bishop North himself points beyond such language, the use of the term 'for the poor' runs the risk of perpetuating the myth of passivity in the face of economic injustice which has given rise to such stark inequality. Our language must not further such patterns. Sam Wells has suggested we move beyond language 'for the' poor and towards language 'with'.[67] God is not for us, he is with us. This is a good start, but only goes so far.

If we are to take seriously the preferential option for the poor and begin to redress the economic marginalization of many people and communities in our society, we must lead by example in our patterns of language and terminology of ministry. In order to alleviate the suffering of Christ's body caused by such poverty (including but not limited to economic poverty), we must seek to become a Church that does not act *for* but *with* those economically marginalized and otherwise overlooked. However, we must also go further, not just acting with them but being 'of them'.

A preferential option for the poor includes a genuine listening to the marginalized, but it must also include an adaption on our part. We must become a Church which is the property of the marginalized (of all forms). A Church which puts the poor first in our structures and decision-making processes. A Church which is sensitive to and reflects their concerns and sufferings. More importantly, we must be a Church 'of the marginalized' – intentionally raising up leaders from within these marginalized groups, especially the economically marginalized. To do this may require some deep reflection on our own patterns of leadership and discipleship, and may also lead to some profound changes in the way in which we conceive of growing the Church.

The remainder of this book is devoted to the action we must take together if we are to apply the insights of Catholic Social Teaching.

Notes

1 *Sollicitudo*, 42.
2 *Rerum*, 23.
3 *Rerum*, 28.
4 *Rerum*, 29.
5 *Rerum*, 4.
6 *Rerum*, 24.
7 *Rerum*, 24.
8 *Rerum*, 24.
9 *Rerum*, 24.
10 *Rerum*, 37.
11 Aquinas, *Summa Theologica* II.II.57–8.
12 Finnis, J. M., 'Aquinas on ius and Hart on Rights: A Response to Tierney' in *The Review of Politics* 64.3 (Summer, 2002), 407–10 suggests a basic similarity between modern notions of 'rights' and that referred to by St Thomas. Finnis' view has changed since the publication of his *Natural Law and Natural Rights* (Oxford: Oxford University

Press, 1980) in which he treats the notions as similar but distinct. The real distinction is in the metaphysical framework underpinning a Thomist worldview. Such a framework is not presupposed in modern rights discourse.

13 *Quadragesimo*, 137.

14 *Quadragesimo*, 4.

15 *Quadragesimo*, 7.

16 *Quadragesimo*, 25.

17 *Quadragesimo*, 137.

18 *Quadragesimo*, 137.

19 Humphreys, C. F. (afterwards Alexander), *Hymns for Little Children* (London, 1848).

20 *Quadragesimo*, 59.

21 Pope John XXIII in *The Pope Speaks* 8.4 (Spring 1963), 396, cited in Gutiérrez, G. (trans. Inda, C. and Eagleson, J.), *A Theology of Liberation* (London: SCM Press, 1974).

22 *Mater*, 173; this theme is repeated in his later encyclical *Pacem*, 125: 'The wealthier States, therefore, while providing various forms of assistance to the poorer, must have the highest possible respect for the latter's national characteristics and time-honoured civil institutions. They must also repudiate any policy of domination.'

23 *Mater*, 182.

24 *Mater*, 184.

25 *Octogesima*, 15.

26 *Gaudium*, 4.

27 *Gaudium*, 81.

28 *Gaudium*, 1.

29 Gutiérrez, G., cited in Curnow, R., 'Which Preferential Option for the Poor? A History of the Doctrine's Bifurcation' in *Modern Theology* 31.1 (2015).

30 Boff, L. and Boff, C., 'Retrato de Is Anos Da Teologia da Libertacao' in *Revista Eclesiástica Brasileira* 46 (1968), 269, translated in Landon, M., 'The Social Presuppositions of Early Liberation Theology' in *Restoration Quarterly* 47.1 (2005), 13–31, 14.

31 Third General Conference of Latin American Bishops, 'Evangelization at Present and in the Future of Latin America', 707, translated in Eagleson, J. (ed.), *Puebla and Beyond* (New York: Orbis, 1980) and in Spanish here: https://www.celam.org/documentos/Documento_Conclusivo_Puebla.pdf (accessed 28 August 2018).

32 Third General Conference of Latin American Bishops, 'Evangelization', 733.

33 Third General Conference of Latin American Bishops, 'Evangelization', 733.

34 Hartnett, D., 'Remembering the Poor: Interview with Gustavo Gutiérrez' in *America Magazine* (Feb 3, 2003), available at: https://www.americamagazine.org/faith/2003/02/03/remembering-poor-interview-gustavo-Gutiérrez (accessed 28 August 2018).

35 Gutiérrez, G., 'Preferential Option for the Poor' in Nickoloff, J. B. (ed.), *Gustavo Gutiérrez: Essential Writings* (London: Orbis, 1996), 146.

36 Gutiérrez, 'Option', 146.

37 Ormerod, N., *Creation, Grace and Redemption* (New York: Orbis Books, 2007), 55–6.

38 Gutiérrez, G., 'Revelation and Theological Method' in Nickoloff (ed.), *Essential Writings*, 52.

39 Gutiérrez, 'Option', 146.

40 *Laborem*, 8.

41 *Laborem*, 8.

42 *Laborem*, 8.

43 *Sollicitudo*, 42.

44 *Sollicitudo*, 42.

45 *Sollicitudo*, 43.

46 *Sollicitudo*, 42.

47 *Centesimus*, 11.

48 *Centesimus*, 57.

49 *Centesimus*, 57.

50 Centesimus, 57.

51 *Centesimus*, 28.

52 *Compendium*, 182.

53 *Caritas*, 75.

54 Benedict XVI, 'Address to the Inaugural Session of the Fifth General Conference of the Bishops of Latin American and the Caribbean' (13 May 2007), 3, available at: http://w2.vatican.va/content/benedict-xvi/en/speeches/2007/may/documents/hf_ben-xvi_spe_20070513_conference-aparecida.html (accessed 28 August 2018).

55 *Evangelii Gaudium*, 195.

56 *Evangelii Gaudium*, 195.

57 *Evangelii Gaudium*, 198.

58 *Evangelii Gaudium*, 198.

59 Ormerod, *Creation*, 55–6.

60 *Laudato Si'*, 158.

61 *Laudato Si'*, 158.

62 *Who is my neighbour? A letter from the House of Bishops to the People and Parishes of the Church of England for the General Election 2015* (London: Church House, 2015), 61–2.

63 Archbishops of Canterbury and York, *To the Parishes and Chaplaincies of the Church of England* (6 May 2017), 1, available at:

https://www.churchofengland.org/media/3977056/electionletter_text.pdf (accessed 20 December 2017).

64 *To the Parishes*, 2.

65 *Sollicitudo*, 42.

66 *Evangelii Gaudium*, 198.

67 In a number of places, including: http://thecresset.org/2013/Easter/Wells_E2013.html.

8

See, Judge, Act

We are coming towards the end of our survey of Catholic Social Teaching. In this chapter, we begin to consider how we are to apply the insights of Catholic Social Teaching to build communities of human flourishing. Our conclusion, in the following chapter, will round up the threads of our enquiry and consider how every Christian community might promote the flourishing of every person coming through their doors, and how the principles of Catholic Social Teaching might contribute to that flourishing.

In this chapter, we introduce one method of moving from theory to action that is found within Catholic Social Teaching itself. This is the 'see-judge-act' method developed by Joseph Cardijn, whom we met above, and included within official Catholic Social Teaching by John XXIII.

The see-judge-act method calls us to observe the reality of the contemporary situation and the world around us; to judge the situation according to the standards of the Gospel and the teaching of the Church; and to act in such a way as the Gospel demands. One way of thinking of this judgement to action phase is through asking the question: How or on what must I act to bring the world I am observing more in line with the kind of world demanded by the Gospel?

In this chapter we explore the intellectual background of this method. We shall see that far from it being an alien intrusion to Catholic thought, this call to action comes from the same theoretical basis as the rest of Catholic Social Teaching.

In what follows, we see how this method worked within the Young Christian Worker (JOC) communities which first made use of the method. We explore its place within the official documents of Catholic Social Teaching. Finally, we ask how it can inspire and aid us in fulfilling the call to action the Gospel makes on every Christian.

Scriptural Basis

Before considering the theoretical basis of the see-judge-act method, we will consider an example of the method at work within Scripture. Guillermo Cook sees Jesus' interaction with the blind man in John 9 as following the pattern of see-judge-act.

Jesus walks along and *sees* a man blind from birth (John 9.1). His disciples ask whether the man's blindness is a result of his or his parents' sin. Jesus *judges*, responding that he is not blind as a result of sin, but that his blindness is part of his vocation before God, 'that God's works might be revealed in him' (John 9.2–3). Jesus *acts*, rubbing a paste of mud and saliva on the man's eyes, and telling him to go and wash in the pool. The man comes back able to see (John 9.6–7).

Cook sees a model of the see-judge-act method at work in this interaction: 'Jesus has seen the blind man. He has judged his situation, and has acted in his favour. One more person has been incorporated into the kingdom of God.'[1]

There are more features of this passage which help us to see how the see-judge-act method might help us put the principles of Catholic Social Teaching into practice. These features help us both put the principles into practice and consider the reaction from others as we do so.

First, we notice something important about the 'judgement' stage Cook has identified within John 9. Jesus judges as a result of the disciples' questions, which he then discusses with them.

When we observe a situation, it is sometimes the questions of others who have observed the same situation which prompt us towards discerning the right course of action. Moreover, we see that judging the right course of action is often a task which happens in deliberation with others.

Second, we note the potential results of our action. Jesus acts and restores the sight of the man born blind. The restoration of the sight causes incredulity (John 9.8–12, 18–21). An action designed to bring about change in a difficult situation might be judged according to the prevailing norms of the day and rejected as impossible or impractical according to that system, while being demanded of those following Christ. The man whose sight has been restored is brought before the religious authorities of the day by the crowds who do not rejoice that the man's sight has been restored, but condemn Jesus for violating the normal practice of Sabbath observance (John 9.16).

This alerts us to the fact that acting, having observed the reality of the contemporary situation, and judging how best to act while following Christ, is rarely an easy path. It can upset those who maintain the status quo, and can lead to the rejection of those who act, and those liberated by the action. The blind man is driven out of community (John 9.34).

Cook unpacks further the consequence of such action. 'Seeing, judging and acting require discernment, critical criteria and consistent action when we have to choose between several alternatives of pastoral action. If we follow along Jesus' way, our ministry will develop a critical dimension and take on a prophetic quality as we confront false social, political, and religious options, particularly those that we will discover in our own church traditions.'[2]

We are reminded that sometimes acting will not be easy, or comfortable. This is especially true as we engage in the difficult task of confronting 'false social, political, and religious options', which are often defended by the powerful and vested interests whose own standing benefits from the preservation of these false options.

In all our action, we are called to live out that love with which Christ loved us. Such loving action is rarely welcomed, and is often driven out, precisely because of its threat to the status quo, vested interests and the 'powers that be'. Herbert McCabe notes that if we act rightly in accordance with this love, we will almost certainly be rejected: 'If you love enough you will be killed. Humankind inevitably rejects the only solution to its problem, the solution of love. Human history rejects its own meaning.'[3]

Prudence

The see-judge-act method is sometimes spoken of with suspicion in more conservative Catholic circles as being an external intrusion from other ideologies. It bears resemblance to methodologies of reflective praxis arising out of Liberation Theology. It comes from Cardinal Cardijn's JOC movement, which from earliest days was regarded with suspicion by some as being a cover for socialism with a daily Mass.

It is true that the see-judge-act method bears similarities with those methodologies of reflective practice arising out of Liberation Theology; for example, Paolo Freire's famous *Pedagogy of the Oppressed*. Freire does incorporate elements of Marxist analysis to help develop his pedagogy. His combination of action and reflection does have resemblances to Cardijn's see-judge-act method. Freire writes: 'Functionally, oppression is domesticating. To no longer be prey to its force, one must emerge from it and turn upon it. This can be done only by means of the praxis: reflection and action upon the world in order to transform it.'[4] Throughout, he describes a constant cycle of action, reflection, action, which finds its fruition in the countless cycles of theological reflection which exist today (few, if any, of which result in the kind of liberating praxis envisaged by Freire). However, these similarities have little or nothing to do with the see-judge-act methodology as articulated by Cardijn, and subsequently included within Catholic Social Teaching.

The source from which Cardijn derives the see-judge-act method is none other than Thomas Aquinas. Once again, St Thomas proves himself to be the source of this aspect of Catholic

Social Teaching, as he has been the source of so much of the social teaching we have encountered throughout this book.

The earliest reference to the see-judge-act method occurs in a pamphlet written in 1930, entitled 'The Young Christian Worker Movement and the Intellectual and Moral Distress of Young Workers', in which Cardijn writes: 'To learn to *act*, after having learnt to *see* and to *judge*, this the goal always aimed at in every jocist enquiry, in every discussion and in every conversation.'[5]

When we turn to St Thomas, we see the see-judge-act method is present in his discussion of the virtue of prudence. Aquinas argues that 'it belongs to prudence rightly to *counsel*, *judge*, and *command* concerning the means of obtaining a due end, it is evident that prudence regards not only the private good of the individual, but also the Common Good of the multitude'.[6] Aquinas' understanding of prudence which *counsels*, *judges* and *commands* with respect to the Common Good is the source of Cardijn's see-judge-act method.[7] What is to Aquinas *counsel*, *judge*, *command* becomes for Cardijn *see-judge-act*.

What was for Aquinas a theological understanding of prudence, becomes for Cardijn a methodology by which to inspire the youth involved in the JOC. Mary Zotti notes how this method operated within the JOC: 'Using the method of Observe-Judge-Act, they [members of the JOC] looked at the realities of their lives, judged whether their observations were in line with the teachings of Jesus Christ, and then took action.'[8]

Cardijn himself describes this method in more detail, and his hopes for the JOC movement: 'Leaders and members learning to see, judge, and act; to see the problem of their temporal and eternal destiny to judge the present situation, the problems, the contradiction, the demands of an eternal and temporal destiny; to act with a view to the conquest of their temporal and eternal destiny. To act individually and collectively, in a team, in a local section, in a regional federation, in a national movement, in meetings, in achievement, in life and in their environment, forming a single front, going forward to the conquest of the masses of their fellow-workers.'[9]

See-Judge-Act in Catholic Social Teaching

Cardijn's methodology would become a feature of Catholic Social Teaching through its incorporation by John XXIII in *Mater et Magistra*. In that encyclical he writes: 'There are three stages which should normally be followed in the reduction of social principles into practice. First, one reviews the concrete situation; secondly, one forms a judgement on it in the light of these same principles; thirdly, one decides what in the circumstances can and should be done to implement these principles. These are the three stages that are usually expressed in the three terms: look, judge, act.'[10]

John XXIII goes on to commend this method as a means of translating theory into action, especially for the young. He notes that: 'Knowledge acquired in this way does not remain merely abstract, but is seen as something that must be translated into action.'[11]

The Second Vatican Council instructs the faithful in a manner which has echoes of the see-judge-act method. *Gaudium et Spes* notes that: 'It is the task of the entire People of God, especially pastors and theologians, to hear, distinguish and interpret the many voices of our age, and to judge them in the light of the divine word.'[12]

We might think that this is the limit of the impact of Joseph Cardijn's see-judge-act method on Catholic Social Teaching. However, the Compendium of Social Doctrine includes an important section on 'acting with prudence' which both reaffirms the role of the see-judge-act method within Catholic Social Teaching, and makes clear the debt which this method owes to the writing of St Thomas.

The *Compendium* instructs the lay faithful to 'act according to the dictates of prudence'.[13] In doing so, it identifies 'three distinct moments as prudence is exercised' which correspond to Cardijn's see-judge-act method: 'The first moment is seen in the reflection and consultation by which the question is studied and the necessary opinions sought. The second moment is that of evaluation, as the reality is analysed and judged in the light of God's plan. The third moment, that of decision, is based on the preceding steps and makes it possible to choose between the different actions that may be taken.'[14]

The see-judge-act method has been criticized for lacking a final reflective component that discerns whether the action taken, and the judgement made, was correct. This criticism is fair, but neglects the fact that the see-judge-act method is not envisaged in isolation or as a one-off application of Catholic Social Teaching. The see-judge-act method is intended as a constant feature of the life of the moral agent, as we see in its theoretical basis in the writings of St Thomas. Moral agents are not expected to be prudent occasionally, but always. Likewise, the method of see-judge-act is a constant attempt to apply the principles of Catholic Social Teaching to everyday life.

Individuals will fail to apply see-judge-act correctly in many instances. Such failures are inevitable. The see-judge-act method, arising out of the virtue of prudence, calls for the constant reapplication of see-judge-act to discern the right, and prudential, action in every circumstance. This includes when an individual has wrongly applied the see-judge-act method. They are not called to give up the method, but to reapply see-judge-act in the hope that they might act more clearly in line with the principles of Catholic Social Teaching the next time they act.

Seeing, Judging, Acting Today

What does this method look like in practice? Three examples will help us as we consider how the see-judge-act method might be employed today. These are community organizing, payday lending and human trafficking. Community organizing demonstrates a similar method of practical action. Payday lending and human trafficking give us two contemporary examples of where Churches have 'seen, judged and acted'. This action has effectively helped to make some parts of the world to be a little more closely in line with the principles of Catholic Social Teaching, and so, we hope, God's will for his people.

Judgement is perhaps the most crucial stage. We 'see' a situation by observing the world around us, and noticing the reality of the conditions experienced by all those who share that world with us. How do we judge when to act and what constitutes right action?

An example from the practice of community organizing helps us here. Community organizing is a set of tools and practices for social action developed during the civil rights movement by Saul Alinsky.[15] Lawrence Engel demonstrates that Alinsky himself is an important influence within Catholic social action, particularly in the United States.[16] Alinsky's influence secured Catholic support and finance for a range of community organizing projects. He also had a strong friendship with the theologian Jacques Maritain, who was influential on Catholic thinking during the latter part of the last century.[17]

Community organizing makes use of a similar method of practical action to see-judge-act, namely 'research-action-evaluation'. The evaluation component is designed to prevent needless repetition of ineffective action. Matthew Bolton describes the role evaluation plays 'in creating a group of people who grow in their understanding about what works and what doesn't'.[18] While there is no explicit evaluative component to see-judge-act, in practice, a similar evaluation of past action takes place during the 'judgement' stage. We are encouraged to 'judge' whether an action would be effective based on past experience.

Community organizing also furnishes us a further example of how the judgement stage of see-judge-act works in practice. Community organizers talk of the 'world as it is' and the 'world as it should be'.

Former President Barack Obama worked as a community organizer in Chicago before entering national politics. Michelle Obama described how he used to talk about the 'world as it is' and the 'world as it should be': 'Barack stood up that day, and spoke words that have stayed with me ever since. He talked about "The world as it is" and "The world as it should be." And he said that all too often, we accept the distance between the two, and settle for the world as it is – even when it doesn't reflect our values and aspirations. But he reminded us that we know what our world should look like. We know what fairness and justice and opportunity look like.'[19]

Seeing the reality of the 'world as it is', judging according to a vision for the 'world as it should be' gives us one way of understanding how the see-judge-act method might work in practice.

Our vision for the 'world as it should be' is that set out in Scripture and the teaching of the Church. The 'world as it should be' has been the subject of the whole of this book. A world where human dignity is promoted, the Common Good is furthered, we live in solidarity with one another in a diverse and flourishing society, where systems serve the entire human family and the poor are lifted up from whatever their poverty may be.

Judging how the world currently fails to look like the 'world as it should be' means that we build a plan to act which helps nudge the 'world as it is' towards the 'world as it should be'. Our actions should help overcome the ways the world currently isn't ordered according to God's will for us, where the principles of Catholic Social Teaching aren't followed. Our actions should help bring about ways of living and being in community that more closely resemble God's will for us, and where the principles of Catholic Social Teaching flourish. The world may never be entirely as it should be in this life, but it can be a little more as it should through prudent action. We are not trying to bring about a new world which may never exist, but, as Bolton notes, acting in such a way that we take those 'incremental steps that edge us closer to the world as it should be'.

We can give two examples of where Christian communities have taken such steps. The Church's efforts to reduce those trapped in cycles of payday lending in Britain, and the global effort to conquer the evil of human trafficking are examples where the Church has seen, judged and acted.

After the financial crisis of 2008, payday lending saw increasing numbers of people trapped in cycles of consumer debt. Payday loans companies would offer quick access to cash to plug gaps until payday, while charging exorbitant levels of interest and fees. This often resulted in people being trapped in a cycle of debt from which some may never have escaped. Justin Welby, Archbishop of Canterbury, made this a particular concern of his. He, with others, saw the misery of those trapped in these cycles of debt, judged how best he could make use of the assets of the Church of England, and acted accordingly.

A Churches Credit Union was established to offer low-interest loans, and other initiatives started to train people in responsible finance and saving. The Archbishop was frank that he wanted to outcompete the payday lenders, by making access to responsible credit unions much easier, partly through utilizing the network of the thousands of parish churches across the country. The Church was also involved in the successful campaign to legislate for a cap on the amount of interest and fees lenders could charge. Justin Welby, in his *Dethroning Mammon*, notes the success of this action: 'In the UK, membership of credit unions has grown by 123,000 (or 13%) since July 2013 . . . at the same time, volume of payday lending in the UK has declined 68% from its peak in 2013, and Citizens Advice reports a 53% drop in the number of payday loan problems they helped between April and June 2015 compared to the same period in 2014. We can make a difference.'[20]

Another example of see-judge-act in action is the action taken by the Roman Catholic Church in England and Wales in relation to human trafficking. Pope Francis has described human trafficking as 'an open wound on the body of contemporary society, a scourge upon the body of Christ. It is a crime against humanity.'[21] Cardinal Vincent Nichols, Archbishop of Westminster (successor to Cardinal Manning we encountered above), with the Catholic Bishops of England and Wales has taken the initiative to act together against human trafficking. These Church leaders have seen the problem of trafficking as it destroys the lives of the individuals trafficked within our society. They have acted by calling together a conference of international experts and law enforcement officials to combine plans for action 'accompanied and reinforced by the mercy of the Gospel, by closeness to men and women who are victims of this crime'.[22]

Judged against the authentic human freedom demanded by the Gospel, this network of Catholics and international experts committed to act together against human trafficking. They signed the Santa Marta commitment, which makes clear that this action against human trafficking is a concrete example of Catholic Social Teaching in practice. The signatories exhorted 'the international community to adopt an even more unanimous and effective strategy against human trafficking, so that in every part of the world, men and women may no longer be used as a means to an end, and that their inviolable dignity may always be respected'.[23] We see the principle of the inviolable dignity of every person generating action, when Catholics have seen that trafficking violated that dignity and then judged how best to act. The Santa Marta Group formed as a result continues to act against human trafficking by bringing different experts and law enforcers together to develop creative strategies to tackle the evil of people trafficking.[24]

Both the Church of England's action on payday lending, and the Roman Catholic Church's action on trafficking, offer us two concrete examples of how see-judge-act works in practice. Situations which lead to misery and despair are observed, creative action is decided upon through judging their situation against the demands of the Gospel and the principles found in Catholic Social Teaching, and concrete action taken to bring about an end to the situation of misery for those involved.

Many more examples could be given of such action in practice. We now turn to our final chapter, to bring the threads of our study together. We've seen in this chapter how Catholic Social Teaching might be applied to situations of despair. In our final chapter we ask what our churches and Christian communities might look like if we are intentional about ordering them with the principles of Catholic Social Teaching in mind.

Notes

1 Cook, G., 'Seeing, Judging, Acting: Evangelism in Jesus' Way' in *International Review of Mission* 87.346 (July 1998), 388–96, 395.

2 Cook, 'Seeing, Judging, Acting', 396.

3 McCabe, H., 'Good Friday: The Mystery of the Cross' in *God Matters* (London: Continuum, 2005).

4 Freire, P., *Pedagogy of the Oppressed* (London: Bloomsbury, 1992) (orig. 1970).

5 Gigacz, S., 'Found! Cardijn's "lost" See Judge Act Article of 1914', available at http://cardijnresearch.blogspot.com/2013/02/found-cardijns-lost-see-judge-act.html?q=see+judge+act (accessed 28 August 2018).

6 Aquinas, *Summa Theologica*, II.II.47.10.

7 For possible Thomist influences on Cardijn, see Gigacz, S., 'Seek, Judge, Act – the Sertillanges side of the story', available at: http://cardijn-research.blogspot.com/2012/10/seek-judge-act-sertillanges-side-of.html?q=see+judge+act (accessed 27 August 2018).

8 Zotti, M., 'The Young Christian Workers', in *U.S. Catholic Historian* 9.4 (1990), 387–400, 387.

9 Cardijn, J. in *Semaine d'Etudes Internationale de la JOC 25–29 aout 1935* (Brussels: 1935), trans. Langdale, E., available at www.josephcardijn.com/the-three-truths (accessed 11 August 2015).

10 *Mater*, 236.

11 *Mater*, 237.

12 *Gaudium*, 44.

13 *Compendium*, 547.

14 *Compendium*, 547.

15 For the close relation between community organizing and Catholic Social Teaching, see Ivereigh, A., *Faithful Citizens: A Practical Guide to Catholic Social Action* (London: Darton, Longman & Todd, 2010).

16 Engel, L., 'The Influence of Saul Alinsky on the Campaign for Human Development' in *Theological Studies* 59 (1998), 636–1.

17 Their friendship is documented in a long correspondence, published as Doering, B. (ed.), *The Philosopher and the Provocateur: The Correspondence of Jacques Maritain and Saul Alinsky* (Notre Dame, IN: University of Notre Dame Press, 1994).

18 Bolton, M., *How to Resist: Turn Protest to Power* (London: Bloomsbury, 2018).

19 Obama, M., 'Speech to Democratic National Convention 2008', available at: http://www.npr.org/templates/story/story.php?storyId=93963863 (accessed 28 August 2018).

20 Welby, J., *Dethroning Mammon: Making Money Serve Grace* (London: Bloomsbury, 2016), 156.

21 Pope Francis, 'Address to Participants in the International Conference on Combating Human Trafficking' (10 April 2014), available at: https://w2.vatican.va/content/francesco/en/speeches/2014/april/documents/papa-francesco_20140410_tratta-persone-umane.html (accessed 28 August 2018).

22 Francis, 'Combating Human Trafficking'.

23 Santa Marta Commitment, available at: http://santamartagroup.com/about-santa-marta-group/declaration/ (accessed 28 August 2018).

24 For more information on their work, see: www.santamartagroup.com (accessed 28 August 2018).

9

Flourishing

This chapter brings our introduction to Catholic Social Teaching to its conclusion. In the preceding chapters, we have already begun to draw out practical implications of the principles of Catholic Social Teaching. Throughout, we have attempted to render the structure of Catholic Social Teaching a little less well hidden.[1]

In this final chapter, we set out a vision for how a church or Christian community might embody and live out the principles of Catholic Social Teaching. We do so in the belief that groups of people intentionally living out these principles will provide oxygen for the transformation of the Church and the world.

In each case, we ask how intentionally living the particular principle of Catholic Social Teaching in question might shape the structures and practices of our churches and Christian communities. We consider how the principle might be put into practice in the life of such communities, and how it might lead to the flourishing of that community and the individuals which come into contact with their mission and witness. These are all suggestions of what communities organized around these principles might look like, with which many may find fault and strike many as overly idealized. However, even beginning to discuss what such communities might look like, and thinking through how the principles apply in each and every context, is an important first step in living out the principles of Catholic Social Teaching.

Before doing so, however, we consider the importance of Catholic Social Teaching at the present time. The world seems to be increasingly divided between irreconcilable opposites: Democrat and Republican; Conservative and Labour; Leave or Remain in the European Union; for and against the levels of immigration. We begin by looking at the ability of Catholic Social Teaching to find consensus in the midst of considerable division.

Catholic Social Teaching: An Important Witness

The whole tradition of Catholic Social Teaching begins with the need to seek consensus in the midst of opposing extremes. Leo XIII writes *Rerum Novarum* in order to mediate between the divides opening up within industrialized Europe at the end of the nineteenth century, between 'the enormous fortunes of some few individuals, and the utter poverty of the masses'.[2] He does so in the midst of 'the conflict now raging' in part, to stem 'the spirit of revolutionary change'.[3]

We saw above in the chapter on the Common Good how Catholic Social Teaching negotiated a path between the absolute right to private property, and the pressure of communist calls for the abolition of private property. The position articulated within Catholic Social Teaching achieves a consensus between these two extremes. Private property is permitted as the best means of administration, but all property is destined for common use.

Likewise, we saw how Catholic Social Teaching responded to two insights of Liberation Theology. The preferential option for the poor and the concept of social sin are both included within Catholic Social Teaching but in a more nuanced way than their original form within Liberation Theology. Catholic Social Teaching remains sceptical about ascribing sinful agency to a structure and not to individuals. It recognizes that the poor make a demand on the resources of the rich, but it rejects discrimination against others in prioritizing the interests of the poor.

John Carr calls this process of finding consensus and discerning truth between extremes 'in the often ideological and polarized economic debate . . . "the Catholic AND"'.[4] Carr's 'Catholic AND' is the feature of Catholic Social Teaching which 'brings together complementary ideas and values into a more coherent and integrated framework'.[5] For example, 'private property is both a right *and* a responsibility, there is both a duty to work *and* a right to decent work, wages etc.'.[6]

The just or living wage is a concrete example of this search for consensus between possible extremes. Catholic Social Teaching neither allows free reign for employers to set exploitative wages, nor does it call for wages that are so high they risk unemployment. The call for a living wage is a safeguard against exploitation, while securing dignity for the worker without calling for such a high minimum wage that it risks unemployment. The call for a living wage is a call for the minimum recognition of human dignity that 'wages ought not to be insufficient to support a frugal and well-behaved wage-earner'.[7]

The ability of Catholic Social Teaching to find consensus across divided positions, and to seek truth among extremes, means that it offers important lessons for negotiating the current divided societies in which we live. The documents of Catholic Social Teaching demonstrate how keeping in mind certain foundational principles of decency and dignity can negotiate divides and find ways through extremes. It does not allow a free-for-all, or support of whichever position is popular or politically expedient. Instead, it seeks consensus by applying an agreed set of foundational concerns and ideas to the changing problems of living in the world.

Catholic Social Teaching has shown itself to be an important witness in how to negotiate living and leading in a divided society. It encourages us to hold fast to a small number of core principles essential to our faith, and to show as much flexibility as we are able in our application of these core principles to the many and changing social problems we face. In so doing, it shows us the importance of finding a consensus which is not simply the whim of a majority, or that excludes some or part of society from its scope, but seeks to discern truth among the many conflicting and divided voices of our day.

Dignity

We now turn to consider what it might look like to organize a church or Christian community according to each of the principles of Catholic Social Teaching we have explored. The first of these is the inviolable dignity of the human being. What might it look like to be part of a Christian community founded on this inviolable dignity?

A Christian community which safeguards and promotes the inviolable human dignity of every person will not be content with activities or programmes which presume to know the needs and concerns of people that come across its threshold. A community which recognizes and promotes human dignity will devise activities and programmes that arise out of the needs and concerns of the particular human beings that make up their community. They will be active in discerning these needs and concerns by establishing methods and structures of discerning those needs.

Matthew Bolton once described the business of parish ministry as the 'radical task of empathy' with each and every person who comes through the door of the church.[8] Clergy and lay leaders will not imagine they know the needs and concerns of the whole of the community, but will cultivate this 'radical empathy'. They will encourage and develop the whole community to articulate those needs and concerns themselves.

A Christian community which respects the human dignity of every person will not instrumentalize any employee or volunteer. They will not be judged merely by the service they perform. As much as is possible, individuals will not be seen as candidates to fill slots on rotas. Instead, rotas will be devised out of the interests and concerns of those presenting themselves as volunteers, and the needs perceived by the community as a whole.

A Christian community which respects the human dignity of every person will work with each person to ensure they have means to develop and articulate their Christian service and faith. They will meet regularly to agree a trajectory of involvement in order to deepen their participation in this community and contribute to their flourishing. Together, the person and the leaders of the community will discern how, and in what ways, God is calling them into flourishing through this community. They will discern what skills it is that God is calling the person to develop, and how and in what ways the community is called to change in order to allow the flourishing of this person.

Most important of all, the community will find ways of drawing the individual into the life of prayer, not as a passive consumer of the worship 'product'. Rather, the community will enhance the dignity of the person by discerning ways in which the person can be encouraged as an active disciple and worshipper, through support in learning and nourishing their faith, and lively participation in the sacramental life.

> Key question for a community organized to promote human dignity: Do we discern and promote the particular means of flourishing of each and every person with whom we come into contact?

Common Good

We have seen above that the Common Good involves both a commitment to the good of everyone in a society and also a commitment towards the universal destination of goods. A Christian community that serves and encourages the Common Good will cultivate the same attitude to private property we have seen in the documents of Catholic Social Teaching. They will recognize the universal destination of all their goods.

In practical terms, this means that the community will avoid thinking of buildings or assets as primarily 'theirs'. Instead, they will think of them as tools given to them by God and destined to be put to use for the Common Good. They will be active in discerning how it is God is calling them to use the assets with which they have been entrusted. Initially, this might involve asking how the assets entrusted to our stewardship can be used to support the Christian community in their own use of assets for the Common Good. Eventually the circle will be widened to ask how God is asking us to use the assets for the benefit of each and every person who crosses our threshold.

The Church will reflect carefully before supporting any practical action in the community. When action is supported, it will be judged according to the principle of the Common Good. Key questions will be whether anyone in our community, or beyond, will be harmed by proceeding with this or that action. If the aim of the action seems to be for the good of most of the community, but it becomes clear that some individuals will be harmed through this path of action, this does not simply mean the community should object to the action. Instead, they are called to ask how might the same or similar aims be achieved which avoids harm to those individuals? How can those individuals come to share in the intended positive outcomes of such action?

Above all else, communities flourishing according to the Common Good cannot be jealous. They are called to ask whether they are the best custodians of the assets or skills which have been entrusted to their community. Are they called to share skills or assets for the building up of another community, perhaps to the detriment of their own? Are they called to support the flourishing of a way of being Church or human which looks very different or is even strongly at odds with their own?

> Key question for a community organized to promote the Common Good: How are we exercising our stewardship of the goods and assets that God has entrusted to us, and whose claim on those assets are we failing to hear?

Solidarity

Richard Gillard's modern hymn 'Brother, sister, let me serve you' is often sung at services in which clergy are appointed or installed to a new post.[9] It includes the stanza: 'I will weep when you are weeping; when you laugh I'll laugh with you; I will share your joy and sorrow till we've seen this journey through.'

This is one version of the principle of solidarity, based on Paul's notion of the body of Christ in 1 Corinthians: 'If one member suffers, all suffer together with it; if one member is honoured, all rejoice together with it' (1 Cor. 12.26).

A community which recognizes the principle of solidarity will celebrate successes together, and commiserate sorrows. It will especially celebrate and rejoice in the joys and successes of the least within their community, and especially provide support during their losses and sufferings. A community of solidarity will see the rich and poor alike stand together in the many trials and tribulations of the Christian life, and nurture each other in their discipleship.

A community of true solidarity will see rich and poor alike share each other's joys and sorrows, so much so they will cease to regard each other as anything other than fellow members of Christ's body. The commitment to the Common Good of the wealthier sections of the community will be such that any divide between them will become small indeed.

Another hymn, sung less often to mark the arrival of new clergy, is G. K. Chesterton's 'O God of Earth and Altar'. It puts the principle of Christian solidarity rather more starkly than Gillard's vision of solidarity. Chesterton's hymn calls on God to 'tie in a living tether, the prince and priest and thrall, bind all our lives together, smite and save us all'.

A community which lives according to the principle of solidarity will realize that all divides within the community are merely apparent. Solidarity becomes an active part of community life, constantly seeking to build up the weaker members of the community, while constantly guarding against the more powerful safeguarding their vested interests or abusing their wealth at the expense of the weaker members of the community.

A community of solidarity knows that they all suffer when the poorest suffer, they know that they are all built up when the divides between rich and poor are overcome. They know that their unity in Christ, and solidarity in humanity, means more than their division in social or financial status. They know that their solidarity means that their fates are entwined together, and not to act on behalf of their brother or sister would be a failure to act for themselves. They long for such divisions to subside. They long to see Chesterton's prayer realized: 'In ire and exultation, aflame with faith, and free, lift up a living nation, a single sword to thee.'

> Key question for a community organized to promote the principle of solidarity: Whose voice isn't being heard and how do we relate to people who aren't like us?

Subsidiarity

A community which lives according to the principle of human dignity as we outline above, will be a community which lives according to the principle of subsidiarity. Subsidiarity is a key tool in the promotion of human dignity.

'Vertically', it means that decisions are made by or as close to those who are affected by them as possible. 'Horizontally', it means the promotion of a whole range of intermediary groups and associations where the skills and tools of active participation in the community are acquired and practised.

Subsidiarity is essential to any healthy organization. A parish in which the clergy or significant leaders do everything is not a healthy parish. 'Father knows best' can often be translated as 'Father knows little', since its starves the whole community of the practice of decision-making and active participation in the life of the community. Moreover, it is exhausting for the clergy and leadership (as we saw in the example of Moses) and means that while a small team at the top is working hard and is always very busy, in reality very little ends up getting done and the community can all too easily stagnate.

Clericalism is a potential danger for all those ordained or in active ministry. It is also the greatest threat to subsidiarity operating at community level. Pope Francis has repeatedly spoken out against such clericalism, which 'leads to an excision in the ecclesial body'.[10] Elsewhere he notes how 'excessive clericalism' keeps 'people away from decision-making' and prevents the 'formation needed to take on important responsibilities'.[11] His strongest condemnation of clericalism is found in a letter to the *Pontifical Commission for Latin America*: 'Clericalism, far from giving impetus to various contributions and proposals, gradually extinguishes the prophetic flame to which the entire Church is called to bear witness in the heart of her peoples. Clericalism forgets that the visibility and sacramentality of the Church belong to all the People of God not only to the few chosen and enlightened.'[12]

Subsidiarity is in the lifeblood of many parishes and Christian communities. Opportunities to develop the skills and responsibilities of active participation are found wherever there are associations of people within a larger Christian community – guilds, home groups, cells, sodalities, worship groups, societies, choirs, Sunday schools, even Church councils – can all be places of opportunity to strengthen subsidiarity and build a flourishing community. Active encouragement towards participation and decision-making, where decisions are substantial and people are genuinely listened to and involved, is key to a community's flourishing. This encourages commitment to the community and its whole flourishing, by encouraging the taking of responsibility for the whole community's welfare by individuals at every level.

Key question for a community organized to promote the principle of subsidiarity: How are decisions made in our community and how do we encourage participation of each and every person?

Structures of Sin

The frightening thing about the sinful structures at work within society is how little we notice them, and how much we take them for granted.

As someone who has made use of next-day home delivery, cheap transportation apps, and bought clothes at unbelievably low prices, it's all too easy to forget that the unbelievably good deal is often exactly that. Unbelievable, because it's not actually a good deal. What looks like a good and convenient deal for us is actually a bad and inconvenient set of assumptions and working practices for those trapped on low pay or working at the coalface of the gig economy.

This is just one example of the many ways of being that can be taken for granted, but are enmeshed in a set of sinful structures arising out of the actions of individuals who have chosen to prioritize the convenience of one set of people over the dignity of another.

The first step for a community that wishes to take account of the structures of sin that operate in society, and to play its part in overcoming them, is to notice them. This is harder than it sounds, because these structures are often so invisible and taken for granted that we struggle to see them for what they are.

A community which wishes to overcome such structures must be active in discerning how each and every decision impacts each and every person. The extent to which we as individuals and communities are embroiled in such structures is considerable. From where coffee and other refreshments served after the service derive, to how we treat our waste and recycling, to how we employ and nurture workers and volunteers, many aspects of Christian ministry and community can find themselves supporting a structure of sin. Communities which wish to overcome such structures will seek ways to avoid becoming embroiled in them, and they will aid those who have been impacted by them. They will seek to break open such structures, or establish alternative virtuous structures to avoid them wherever possible.

This is precisely the kind of action we saw promoted by the Archbishop of Canterbury in the last chapter. Churches which wished to break open the sinful structure of the payday loan and cycles of consumer debt established their own virtuous structure of responsible lending and financial advice.

A community which wishes to overcome structures of sin will seek to find similar ways of establishing such virtuous structures, which break open the sinful structure and lead to their demise.

> Key question for a community organized to take account of the structures of sin: To what do we give our support? What are the unintended consequences of our assumptions and what we take for granted, and who is impacted by them?

For the Poor

There are few Christian communities who are not already committed in some way to the poorest in society. However, often this commitment is limited to charity and good deeds.

The option for the poor is more than a commitment to donate to alleviate the suffering of those in financial or material poverty. It is a commitment to tackle the situations and systems which give rise to that poverty. The preferential option for the poor demands more than generosity of giving.

A community which wishes to exercise the preferential option for the poor is a community which asks what changes need to be made to move from a church which helps the poor to a church which is truly of them.

A community which wishes to exercise the preferential option for the poor asks itself how it too contributes to the poverty of others. It asks what assumptions and practices of our community serve to marginalize others and keep those in poverty. It asks not just what can we do to allow the poor to be included and represented. It asks what is needed of us so that the church is a place where poverty is overcome, where those in poverty are in the church, and the church is theirs.

Such an inclusion of the poor might be painful for many of those already within church leadership or in positions of authority. Many of the styles of leadership and patterns of success we are used to are the styles of leadership and patterns of success of the wealthy. A 'successful' poor church might not look like a church which is regarded as successful today, where success is often measured in worldly terms by numbers and financial resources.

Ultimately, a Church of the poor is a Church attentive to the voice of God in those to whom he is close: the poor themselves, those whom history has marginalized, those outside the patterns of decency and respectability that the rich have written for themselves.

> Key question for a community organized to promote the option for the poor: How do we support those in poverty beyond mere charity? How do we respond to God's challenge to us through those marginalized by our current ways of living?

See, Judge, Act

A flourishing community is a community which acts. The 'see-judge-act' method is just one method of engaging in the world, and turning core beliefs into practical action.

A flourishing community is firstly a community which sees. It recognizes the reality of its own practices, blind spots and working assumptions. It recognizes the reality of the society and wider community in which it is found. It looks hard at the community around it, and is active in discerning the truth of any given situation.

A flourishing community is a community which exercises judgement. It is critical in discernment, and active in learning and developing itself in the faith. This means both being attentive in reading Scripture and the tradition. It also means being attentive to God in prayer and especially in the sacraments. Such a community will regularly articulate a vision for the 'world as it should be', and persistently deepen this vision in light of its newfound understanding. It will be deliberate in asking how God's vision for the world, and God's call to serve the world, require it to act.

A flourishing community is a community which acts. Not content with blaming others, or leaving others to act on behalf of those who are suffering, it will seek ways to act where its judgement has determined that something must be done. It will constantly ask 'How are we able to act?' and 'What do we have to do to be able to act more effectively in future?'.

Key question for a community which sees, judges and acts: Who needs us, what is it in our power to do and how are we going to do it?

Flourishing

One of the best ways to think about how the principles of Catholic Social Teaching contribute to the flourishing of a Christian community is to think about what communities might look like where none of the principles are observed: a church where dignity was violated, in the interests of a few, by a centralized leadership, in truck with the authorities of the day, that does nothing to alleviate the suffering of others. Many

Christians would struggle to identify such an organization as a church. We might hope and pray that no such church exists.

Many, if not most, churches and Christian communities are places of flourishing. Many, if not most, churches and Christian communities are places where the light of Christ is seen clearly, and a community transformed by that light, goes out and transforms others. There are, however, plenty of churches and Christian communities which are not truly flourishing, and are not places of true flourishing for others. They are places where not every person enjoys life lived in all its fullness (John 10.10). These might be small, faithful, worshipping communities. These might be hugely successful 'mega-churches'. Perhaps without realizing, they lose focus of one or other of the principles of Catholic Social Teaching.

They might have become overly centralized, where worshippers are passive recipients of a product: the sacrament or the sermon. They might have focused only on serving the needs and interests of a particular section of their community, the section with which the leadership feels most comfortable and looks most like them. They might have become a community which feels hard-pressed by church authorities and the world outside, and have become introverted and inward looking, having forgotten how to act and live out their faith.

Catholic Social Teaching reminds us that flourishing is a process which requires us to be active and intentional. Likewise, each of the principles must be lived out actively and intentionally. Pope John XXIII reminded us of this in his call to wealthy nations to take 'positive steps to pool their material and spiritual resources', when he entitled that section of his encyclical 'active solidarity'.[13] Flourishing, like solidarity, can't be taken for granted. It must be active.

The key to unlocking flourishing of any kind is the freedom we enjoy in Christ. All of our effort as Christians should be in response to that freedom, and as a means to share that freedom ever more widely. This means, as Paul VI wrote, 'building a human community where men can live truly human lives, free from discrimination on account of race, religion or nationality, free from servitude to other men or to natural forces which they cannot yet control satisfactorily. It involves building a human community where liberty is not an idle word.'[14] A flourishing community takes nothing for granted. A flourishing community is an active one, where human flourishing itself is not an idle set of words.

Indifference

This brings our discussion of the principles of Catholic Social Teaching to an end. One of the aims of this book, and of this last chapter especially, has been to encourage Christians and Christian communities to be places where the principles of Catholic Social Teaching are more actively lived out. It is hoped that reflecting on Catholic Social Teaching might encourage all Christian communities in their vocation to become flourishing communities inspired to act.

The biggest challenge to action is indifference. We are encouraged toward indifference by the way our society, especially in the modern world, is structured. We are daily encouraged to think there is no other way, and to enjoy a seemingly ever more convenient lifestyle, with all of its rewards and no costs or obligations.

This is one way the 'structures of sin', identified by Catholic Social Teaching, operate, as Mathias Nebel reminds us: 'Structures of sin impose themselves by indifference to injustice and by despair. We know, indeed, that the opposite of love is not hate but indifference – and indifference is what takes over in a malign institution. Indifference comes about with the progressive loss of that relationship to the other which is a condition of our own personhood as well as the only place where personhood can find fulfilment. This is why indifference not only denies love but justice too. If a person is indifferent, structural injustice, the death of an innocent child, will not affect him. This is a deep and terrible enslavement.'[15]

We are reminded by the song from Pope Francis' native Argentina in which the songwriter León Gieco 'only asks of God that I am not indifferent to pain' and that 'death won't find me empty and alone without having done the sufficient'.[16] How do we overcome such indifference? If Nebel is right, and the opposite of indifference is love, the answer is the same as it has been throughout Christian history. Love.

What's needed to bring about a flourishing Church, to live according to the principles of Catholic Social Teaching, to overcome the social ills which gave rise to this rich body of thought, is a greater adherence to the command which has been at the centre of the Christian life since its inception. We are called to love, because we have been loved.[17]

Such love encompasses all of the principles which have been the subject of this book. It respects the dignity of every person, it builds relationship, facilities participation, exalts the lowly, blows open structures of sin.

Such love means that we might have to be willing to give up some of the pleasures and resources we enjoy to see that love more fully realized even in this world. John Paul II puts this best: 'One's neighbour must therefore be loved, even if an enemy, with the same love with which the Lord loves him or her; and for that person's sake one must be ready for sacrifice, even the ultimate one: to lay down one's life.'[18]

Perfect love casts out not only fear, but indifference.[19] With this insight, we can sum up the whole tradition of Catholic Social Teaching, and the principles derived from it, in these simple words: love in action.

Notes

1 Justin Welby notes 'the glorious and – if I may say so to *The Tablet* – far too well-hidden structure of Catholic Social Teaching, which surprisingly few Catholics know about, let alone others' in Lamb, C., 'Archbishop Means Business' in *The Tablet* (November 2012), reproduced at: http://www.thinkinganglicans.org.uk/archives/005744.html (accessed 28 August 2018).

2 *Rerum*, 1.

3 *Rerum*, 1.

4 Carr, J., 'Moving from Research to Action: Some Lessons and Directions (from a Catholic Social Ministry Bureaucrat)' in Finn, D. (ed.), *The True Wealth of Nations: Catholic Social Thought and Economic Life* (Oxford: Oxford University Press, 2010), 341–9, 346.

5 Carr, 'Research to Action', 346.

6 Carr, 'Research to Action', 347.

7 *Rerum*, 45.

8 Author of *How to Resist*, in conversation.

9 Gillard, R., 'The Servant Song' (Kingsway Thankyou Music, 1977).

10 Pope Francis, 'Letter to the People of God' (20 August 2018), available at: http://w2.vatican.va/content/francesco/en/letters/2018/documents/papa-francesco_20180820_lettera-popolo-didio.html (accessed 29 August 2018).

11 *Evangelii Gaudium*, 102.

12 Pope Francis, 'Letter to Cardinal Marc Ouellet President of the Pontifical Commission for Latin America', available at: https://w2.vatican.va/content/francesco/en/letters/2016/documents/papa-francesco_20160319_pont-comm-america-latina.html (accessed 20 August 2018).

13 *Pacem*, 98.

14 *Populorum*, 47.

15 Nebel, M., 'Transforming Unjust Structures: A Philosophical and Theological Perspective' in *Political Theology* 12.1 (2011), 118–43, 138–9.

16 Gieco, L., 'Sólo le pido a Dios' from the album IV LP (Argentina: Music Hall Records, 1978).

17 1 John 4.10–11.

18 *Sollicitudo*, 40.

19 1 John 4.18.

Index of Names

Index of Subjects

Index of Scriptural References